Rethinking Superhero and Weapon Play

Other books by Steven Popper

Join the resolute and beautiful Sanctifier Shenaria Calvert and her steadfast companions, Matthias and Modesty, in this thrilling sci-fi trilogy about the cataclysmic struggle between good and evil.

The Day of Transformation: The First Thrilling Sanctifier Shenaria Calvert Chronicle (2010)

The Night of Decision: The Second Gripping Sanctifier Shenaria Calvert Chronicle (2011)

The Hour of Revelation: The Third Enthralling Sanctifier Shenaria Calvert Chronicle (2012)

Rethinking Superhero and Weapon Play

Steven Popper

 Open University Press

Open University Press
McGraw-Hill Education
McGraw-Hill House
Shoppenhangers Road
Maidenhead
Berkshire
England
SL6 2QL

email: enquiries@openup.co.uk
world wide web: www.openup.co.uk

and Two Penn Plaza, New York, NY 10121-2289, USA

First published 2013

A catalogue record of this book is available from the British Library

ISBN-13: 978-0-33-524706-6 (pb)
ISBN-10: 0-33-524706-7 (pb)
eISBN: 978-0-33-524707-3

Library of Congress Cataloging-in-Publication Data
CIP data applied for

Typesetting and e-book compilations by
RefineCatch Limited, Bungay, Suffolk
Printed and bound by CPI Group (UK) Ltd, Croydon, CR0 4YY

Fictitious names of companies, products, people, characters and/or data that may be used herein (in case studies or in examples) are not intended to represent any real individual, company, product or event.

The *McGraw-Hill* Companies

Praise for this book

"Warm, funny, smart, and honest, the argument made in Steven Popper's book astutely, and with a sharp eye for detail, teases out many subtle reflections on morality, childhood development and the paradoxes of human nature, through the lens of our much-loved Superhero narratives. He is able, through nuanced and well-supported argument, drawn from both theory and practice, and from pedagogy and real life, to present a compelling and detailed account of the ways in which these stories might interface with the moral development of children. The book offers a rich, and articulate narrative of its own, which 'aims at the good' in its desire to propose that immersion in such superhero 'narrative play' can teach children about ethics, social responsibility, and what it is to be 'human'. This is also a wonderful contribution to debates around the role of mass media in promoting critical thinking and enquiry among children."

Dr. Sheena Calvert, Senior Lecturer, University of Westminster, UK

"This book authoritatively assesses the virtues of engaging in superhero play with young children. It argues that far from damaging children and encouraging them to adopt unthinking, aggressive behaviours superhero play is an implicitly moral activity. It encourages children to explore profound moral and ethical thinking. This book is both a well-researched account of the appeal that superhero play has for children of both sexes and a practical guide to how such play can be used imaginatively in early years settings."

Rob Abbott, Senior Lecturer in Early Childhood and Education,
University of Chichester, UK

To my very own trainee superhero, Guy,
and his wonderful mother, Sally: the best wife
and son from here to the planet Krypton

Contents

Preface

Tuesday and Wednesday nights were favourites of mine when I was a child. On Tuesdays I would rush home from school in time to see Adam West's Batman and Burt Ward's Robin go up against that week's dastardly villain and get captured in some fiendish death-trap. On Wednesdays every break-time at school saw me and my friends playing out the events of the show the night before and arguing about how the two heroes would escape. On Thursdays we would continue our happy conversations and play. We all knew that Batman and Robin would always escape and good would always win, but we wanted to see it happen – and be thrilled in the process.

Later, when I was a student, Christopher Reeve made his memorable first appearance as Superman. Here indeed was a hero to look up to. The film seemed to contain not only good versus evil but joy of life and celebration of love. Superman somehow managed to reverse Lois Lane's demise, showing that love was truly stronger than death – much to the delight of the cinema audience who recognized the inherent rightness of this.

Even later, as a nursery and primary school teacher, I utilized superheroes as a tool in the classroom. They were used to engage, inspire and reward children. Issues of good and evil were dramatized and discussed through the medium of superhero stories and scenarios. One year, having run out of reward stickers, I improvised by drawing a smiley Batman face on a good piece of work, with an accompanying speech bubble identifying its particular merits. This went down so well with my Year 2 class that Batman faces became the symbol of approval for the whole year.

More recently, as a university lecturer engaged in early years and primary teacher training, I have used superheroes to draw out and illustrate issues of attachment, children's moral development, questions of nature versus nurture, and even deeper issues about human nature and whether we are predisposed to good or evil simply through being human. All these uses of superheroes seem to have been popular and effective (according to student evaluations) and they appear to have consistently gone down well with the learners who engaged with them.

And yet . . . many of the staff I have worked with over the years have apparently considered my use of superheroes as a quaint idiosyncrasy, perhaps explainable through my being male, or some natural immaturity of mine, rather than a genuinely helpful way of making use of a current cultural resource that is attractive to children and others. In addition, when I became (officially, at least) an academic, I discovered that much of what has been written about children's engagement with superheroes and what has become termed 'war, weapon and superhero play' was quite negative or cautious in tone, and that it in no way matched my own personal experiences of children's engagement with this cultural phenomenon.

This, in a nutshell, is why I have written this book. I wished to explore whether my instinct that children's engagement with war, weapon and superhero play, characters and stories could be a positive and powerful force for good held any water, or whether it was simply a symptom of a nostalgic vision of my own personal enjoyment of them. If children's engagement with war, weapon and superhero play could be of some benefit, then I hoped to be able to suggest how teachers and other educational professionals could realize the potential benefit (especially for children's moral development) that might be available. The result is the book you hold in your hands. I hope you find it useful and enjoy it.

Steven Popper

Acknowledgements

Many people have offered encouragement and creative and helpful suggestions during the composition of this book, and my thanks go to all of them, particularly the children, schools and staff who were generous with their time and support. Special gratitude goes to the following: Fiona Richman, my editor, for her interest, advice and support in turning my initial book proposal into the book you hold here; Madeleine and Sarah Fitzjohn-Scott, for the terrific front cover image that captures the joy of life of superhero play so delightfully; Sheena Calvert and Rob Abbott, for helping me get this book on the right lines in its early stages; Sally Hawkins, Kayleigh Smith, Charlotte Snow, Katrina Jones, Marilyn Duffin and Cheryl Gallon for some very helpful and pleasurable discussions; and Sally Popper, for extremely observant reading, creative ideas and infinite patience.

Last, but not least, huge bat-thanks to my childhood hero, the charming and debonair Adam [Batman] West, for a truly inspiring and utterly delightful hour-long conversation we once shared.

Introduction

> Superman: I remember my father, patient and gentle as we worked the fields together. 'Easy does it', he'd say. 'Scatter the seeds a few at a time. Don't throw them in clumps, let them fall evenly down the rows. Give them enough space. That's the way.' He knew not every seed would make it, but Pa wanted to give each one the chance to grow.
> He used to say the same thing about people – some blossomed right away while others needed a little extra care. It seems I hear my father's voice more clearly at this time of year.
>
> (Dini and Ross 2005/2010: 9)

There is a strong consensus among those who work with children and research their development that children's play is a highly significant vehicle for their investigations of the way the world works, their expressions of ideas and feelings, and their explorations of possibility – in other words, that play is a Good Thing. When it comes to the types of play commonly categorized as 'war, weapon and superhero play', however, there seems to be a more cautious reaction and less consensus of opinion. Literature can be found that talks about war, weapon and superhero play as a good (and possibly even necessary) thing, an understandable thing (but one that requires some adult control or moderation to be of any value), a destructive thing that needs either banning or strictly controlling, or a thing that is really a symptom of other phenomena (such as possible prominent cultural ideas about masculinity and femininity, or inherited evolutionary instincts). Many researchers and commentators in the field have tended to suggest that primary teachers and early years professionals are prone to view war, weapon and superhero play as something with destructive potential, or, at the very least, the potential to distract from any desired learning or behavioural messages that might be on offer.

This book seeks to take a different tack. It aims to explore the cultural and moral stories, characters and scenarios that form much of the basis for war, weapon and superhero play in order to determine exactly *what* it is that children are playing with – in other words, what ideas, moral issues or emotional concerns might fuel and inform such play. It tries to identify what lies behind the appeal that engagement with superheroes and conflict narratives holds for many children (and perhaps not just children, if the current dominance of the cinema by films featuring superheroes and good-versus-evil scenarios is taken into account). Most particularly, it intends to explore the potential impact that engagement with superheroes and war, weapon and superhero play can have on children's developing moral values and sensibilities, and suggest ways in which such potential can be utilized by teachers and other professionals working with children from the early years upwards for the benefit of all: those who blossom right away, and those who need a little extra care.

The book falls into three parts. Part I explores some of the hesitations about war, weapon and superhero play that have been articulated within the educational community, and tries to identify the key arguments raised by some against war, weapon and superhero play. Each of the three chapters in this part explores one of these key arguments against war, weapon and superhero play and tries to suggest a possible answer or alternative perspective to it.

Chapter 1 discusses the viewpoint that engagement with play involving pretend fights or pretend weapons leads to real-life increases in children's aggressive behaviour and outlook, and the not uncommon policy of containing or banning such play. Once the evidence and rationale for this perspective have been discussed, the chapter then explores an alternative way of looking at things by introducing the notion of narrative psychology: how absorbing and playing out stories (including stories that involve war, weaponry or superheroes) allows and enables children to learn about the world and how the people in it (including themselves) tick.

Chapter 2 investigates a perspective that is closely related to that of Chapter 1: that the whole phenomenon of superheroes equates to a cultural promotion of violence; that the twin dynamic of violence and conflict which forms a part of the great majority of superhero stories only serves to put an attractive child-friendly gloss on violent behaviour. The chapter attempts to respond to this perspective by discussing how superhero narratives have an overriding concern with questions of moral responsibility and are therefore more nuanced, thoughtful and potentially valuable to children than might otherwise be the case.

Chapter 3 explores a different sort of objection to war, weapon and superhero play; namely that the male and female role models offered up by superheroes and their narratives are negative, stereotypical and possibly destructive, and the consequent suggested need to either veto or 'correct' children's engagement with them. Once this viewpoint has been discussed, the chapter proposes the alternative perspective that, in fact, superheroes and their narratives can offer up very positive role models for both boys and girls, so children's natural play and interests can be respected and allowed without overt control.

Part II goes beyond these different arguments and attempts to identify what lies beneath children's engagement with superheroes and conflict narratives in the first place. It explores the relationship between different aspects of children's development and significant features of superhero and conflict play and narratives, as detailed below.

Chapter 4 looks in detail at some key understandings of children's moral development, including their development of moral values, moral principles and moral reasoning, and explores some ideas about the nature of morality itself. The chapter then relates these understandings and ideas to ways that superhero characters and scenarios can allow for children's explicit exploration of moral themes and principles, promote their development of moral reasoning, and act as a vehicle for their moral wish-fulfilment.

Chapter 5 discusses the nature of war, weapon and superhero play from a different angle: how the types of activity and behaviour that make up this category of play relate to other forms of play, such as rough-and-tumble play, gendered play, physical play, and play as an outlet for the expression of emotion and the exploration of possibility. In doing so, it attempts to identify reasons for the appeal of war, weapon and superhero play and suggest some benefits that such play might have the potential to offer. The chapter also offers some practical advice designed to help ensure that war, weapon and superhero play (or 'superhero and conflict play', as the chapter begins to define it) does not degenerate into violent or aggressive real-life behaviour.

Chapter 6 explores how superheroes model and promote co-operation, teamwork, camaraderie and empathy for others through scenarios and superhero–team interactions frequently found in superhero narratives. Examples of how superheroes can model loyalty, caring for one another, a sense of community identity, empathy for others, and ways of resolving disagreements are discussed. The chapter then offers some examples of how teachers and early years practitioners can promote and develop children's co-operation and empathy through utilizing superheroes and conflict play in different types of communal activity.

Chapter 7 examines some key understandings of children's development of self-concept and self-esteem. It identifies the importance of high self-esteem and self-actualization for enabling children to flourish and believe in their own potential to grow into and be valuable and valued people. The chapter proceeds to look at how superheroes can be used to offer children strong and reassuring role models of being someone with a strong and definite personal and moral identity and the confidence to be who they are and stand up for what they believe. The chapter concludes by suggesting how the heroic, bold and moral self-actualization modelled and exhibited by superheroes supports and promotes one important key message: that the individual self matters and should be respected and appreciated, and that people's individual moral choices and valuing of themselves and others makes all the difference in the world.

Chapter 8 discusses some key ideas about the essence of morality and moral behaviour. It explores and explains several important approaches to the subject, such as classical dualism (the notion of a division, choice and struggle between good and evil), ideas about the nature of virtue or good character, ideas about the nature of poor or evil character, and the importance of striving for a 'desired good' for all. The chapter then demonstrates how superhero narratives explore all these themes in a focused and definite manner, with a key focus on the need to identify and act upon one's own moral responsibilities, and suggests how superhero narratives can be used to inform children's developing understanding of all these ethical considerations. The chapter concludes by explaining how children's superhero and conflict play often revolves around the key moral themes of enabling freedom, rescuing people from harm or imprisonment, and good overcoming evil.

Parts I and II refer to a large range of superheroes and explore what engagement with them might have to offer children, but in a way that attempts to look at the field as a whole. Part III investigates three particular (and very different) superheroes in detail and depth in order to identify and discuss the exact moral and emotional substance that they and their stories have to offer. Each of the three chapters that make up this part starts by identifying the moral and emotional themes and content that define the particular superhero narratives under discussion, and ends with a series of learning ideas.

Chapter 9 examines the most powerful superhero of all, and explains how his stories revolve around themes of justice, compassion and seeing the best in people, being of good character, and helping those weaker than oneself. The chapter looks at several readings of Superman, notably that he can be seen as a metaphor for God, and identifies the potential for the exploration of some quite profound moral issues as a consequence. The chapter's discussion and proposed learning ideas explain and illustrate how Superman offers children an opportunity to explore ideas about God, the nature and source of goodness, and the just use of power.

Chapter 10 explores a much more emotionally charged figure and shows how his stories are immersed in themes of attachment and loss, human suffering and ideas about human immorality, amorality and evil. The chapter suggests how Batman narratives can be used with children (and older students too) to convey and help illuminate important ethical considerations, such as the moral need to alleviate suffering, differences between justice and vengeance, and the importance of valuing and nurturing the attachment that exists between children and parents.

Chapter 11 discusses how the X-Men and their narratives can help develop children's ideas about inclusive communities and the acceptance and valuing of others who are different than oneself. It explains how the X-Men can be used to inform and increase children's moral thinking about the treatment of different cultural groups by each other, particularly with regard to fear and hatred and ignorance, and can help shed light on some of the worst behaviour of humanity, including Nazism. The chapter shows how exploration of the X-Men's characters and narratives can provide an articulate and valuable opportunity for children to explore ideas about rejection, fear, prejudice, equality, inclusion and standing up for one's rights.

PART I
Arguments held against war, weapon and superhero play – and some responses

1 The argument that war and weapon play almost automatically leads to increased aggression and violence

One of the main reservations that many early years teachers and other educators have about superhero and conflict play is what they see as a central dynamic of violence. It is not just superheroes that seem to cause concern in this regard but much of the content of mass media. Many professionals working with and on the behalf of children seem increasingly worried about the potentially detrimental effects of what is commonly perceived to be an overtly violent content of television programmes, computer games and so on. In a Children's Society report, Layard and Dunn (2009: 60–62) speak for many when they state:

> On television, violence is frequently shown as a part of normal human life (not just a feature of crime or war). The violence is both physical and psychological . . . There is much evidence to suggest that exposure to violent images encourages aggressive behaviour . . . the most dangerous aspect of media content is the lurch towards more and more violence.

The combination of what appears to be an escalation of violent images in the mass media and professional duties towards the behaviour management and moral education of children has led many schools and early years establishments to adopt a policy of non-violence, not only with regard to the treatment of children and staff by one another (which is utterly proper) but also with regard to the imaginative content of children's play. According to Holland (2003) it has become commonplace for educational establishments to adopt a policy of *zero tolerance* towards forms of play that they deem too violent in character:

> A zero tolerance approach to war, weapon and superhero play will be all too familiar to most early years practitioners in this country . . . A zero tolerance approach means that children are not allowed to bring toy weapons into settings, are not allowed to construct or represent

them with found materials and are not allowed to enact war play or superhero scenarios.

(Holland 2003: 2)

What this means in practice is that the *style* of children's play (e.g. making and using pretend guns or swords, or make-believe chasing villains or shooting webs like Spider-Man) is focused on, rather than the *content* of the play. The *substance* or *theme* of the scenario being acted out would not necessarily matter to a professional enforcing a blanket zero tolerance approach. If children are playing out, for example, the defence of a castle, they might be exploring one or more of a whole range of possibilities, such as the need to protect the community or the self from threats, or the attempt to rescue an innocent who has been captured and held prisoner, or even (for older children) the re-creation and exploration of an historical event that they have been learning about.

Similarly, if children have been playing out a struggle between a superhero and a supervillain they might have been playing out ideas of what it is to be heroic or malicious, or dramatizing the attempted capture of a villain who deserves punishment for some imagined crime, or using superpowers to rescue someone from danger. Such play is also likely to include thought and expression about what it is to be good and how power (albeit fantasy 'superpower') could and should be used. For example, during a visit to a school recently, I witnessed two 10-year-old boys in the playground playing out an imaginary Doctor Who scenario of their own devising: the boy playing the alien villain threatened the destruction of buildings and the killing of everyone inside, and taunted Doctor Who for being a coward and not using his own power to stop him, while the boy playing Doctor Who talked of how Doctor Who would not kill. The children were playing out themes of the *differences* between good and evil as well as the *struggle* between them.

But a blanket zero tolerance approach does not allow for consideration of such possibilities. It works on the assumption that, regardless of any other themes that might be at hand, play-acting violence promotes or condones violence, and is therefore to be avoided. According to Levin and Carlsson-Paige (2006: 50):

> With the banning approach, adults tell children they are not allowed to engage in any kind of war and weapons play . . . they feel that allowing the play leads to the development of militaristic attitudes and hurtful behaviour . . . In fact, adults even feel that by banning the play they are actually teaching non-violence, as they take a stand that violence, even when it's pretend, is bad.

This notion, that all play involving pretend violence promotes real violence and aggression – especially if it involves pretend weapons or toy soldiers – has been widespread for a long time. As far back as 1990, Dixon saw such play as the promotion of 'cultural imperialism' and claimed that 'Children in Britain . . . are brought up in a war culture. This is part of a general atmosphere of aggression' (Dixon 1990: 269). Similarly, but much more recently, the General Secretary of the National Union of Teachers, Steve Sinnott, was reported as stating: 'The trouble with weapons is that the toy gun is often accompanied by aggression. The reason why teachers often intervene when kids have toy guns is that the boy is usually being very aggressive' (BBC News 2009). This, of course, is a very genuine worry held by many professionals and deserves proper consideration, and Chapter 5 offers a detailed exploration of this concern and suggests some practical steps that might ensure that such play is prevented from becoming aggressive in real life. In the meantime, however, there do remain two objections to this kind of approach.

First of all, the assumption that all play that involves pretend violence promotes real violence and aggression, or has a direct, causal effect on the children involved in such play is actually rather questionable. The notion that a game involving pretend violence automatically makes the children involved more likely to develop militaristic or violent attitudes is a bit like saying that playing a Postman Pat game makes children more likely to want to work for the Post Office when they grow up. In fact, it has been demonstrated that there is much more to it, and that any blanket assumption of direct causality might miss out on some important psychological understandings of children's behaviour (see below).

The second objection is that the promotion of any moral stance (including that of non-violence) is a much more complex affair than a simple banning approach would seem to recognize. Careful reading of theory and research about children's moral development (see Chapter 4) suggests that the development of any deep-seated moral principles is a sophisticated and slow-burning process over many years (as documented by Kohlberg, Gilligan, Piaget and Coles, among others), and one that is informed by people's stages of cognitive development and their exposure to and reflection about history, literature, religious principles and ethical ideas, and so on. Simply banning a form of expressive play (especially when the content and theme of what is being expressed are not necessarily considered) might run the risk of not actually *teaching* anything substantial – except, of course, that the adults in charge have the power to ban certain types of children's behaviour.

Of course, as mentioned earlier, most British schools do operate a policy of non-violence, and it is quite proper to ban children (and staff) from using actual violence against each other. But to determine that children are so susceptible to the effects of pretend violence that their imaginative play needs this to be automatically edited out of it might be a conclusion that deserves some reconsideration (see Holland 2003). As long as children do not really hurt each other or use genuine violence towards each other, then, perhaps, such play might have a place – and even something positive to offer, as will now be suggested.

Response: Narrative psychology – how children learn through absorbing and playing out stories

The notion that there is a simple causal relationship between children's conflict play and any development of genuinely violent tendencies or attitudes is only sustainable if other factors that might be involved in the children's play are left out of consideration. The reasons for children's engagement with conflict play might need to be considered before any conclusions about its effects can be drawn.

Many of the deeper reasons for children's engagement with conflict play will be explored in detail later in this book; but the simpler reasons deserve to be recognized too. Here are three common reasons for children's engagement with conflict play.

First of all, there is the wish to *share experiences and be involved socially with other children*; in other words, children can be drawn into a game with a conflict scenario simply because that is the available option for pleasing and happy socialization (and also, quite importantly, what Cohen (2006) terms *role reciprocity*; in his example, the taking of turns to chase and be chased). In other words, the *theme* of the game might involve a fictitious conflict between characters or groups on opposing sides, but the actual social dynamic is one of *harmony*, with the children involved in the game taking on and playing out their roles in a way that satisfies and unifies the whole group. This is far removed from any inculcation of aggressive attitudes or behaviour, as the key consideration is keeping the game going well for all participants: the imaginative *content* of the game is quite a different thing from the actual *process* of play that children go through.

A second reason is the wish to *play in a way that symbolizes and expresses self-actualization and the overcoming of causes of potential anxiety* (see Chapter 7). For example, if, during a game played by 5-year-olds, the three little pigs defeat the big bad wolf after two of their houses have been blown down, then what has really been played out is that a threat to home and security has been overcome, and that everything can continue to be all right with the world. Furthermore, it has been the children themselves who have been able to restore order and peace without resorting to adult help. Similarly, if two children are playing *Space Hulk* (Games Workshop's futuristic board game of 2009 which, as the lid of the box says, involves 'man versus alien in desperate battle'), then they are playing out a scenario involving either the protection or the violation of the universe as it is meant to be, and, at the conclusion of the game, both children can claim to have either succeeded in their mission or lulled the enemy into a false sense of security for the *next* thrilling encounter! (The game, of course, has been played in accordance with strict rules; so, once again, the *theme* of the game is conflict, but the *process* of the game involves co-operation and harmony.)

A third common reason behind children's engagement with conflict play is *the appeal that the make-believe characters or narrative scenarios have for them.* If the children adopt the role of a specific pre-existing fictional character, such as Spider-Man or Doctor Who, they do so because these figures have some innate characteristics that appeal to them. Some of these characteristics might be to do with appearance (such as Spider-Man's mask or Batman's cape), some might be to do with the magical powers or devices that such characters commonly use (such as Doctor Who's sonic screwdriver and tardis, Spider-Man's web-shooters, Superman's super-strength or Batman's batmobile) and some might be to do with the *nature of the characters* themselves. As will be discussed throughout this book, many fictional characters appearing in conflict narratives typically model valuable and attractive attributes such as loyalty, determination, resilience, the ability to overcome adversity and a willingness to promote positive outcomes over destructive ones. As an illustration of this, during a recent summer project in a school in Hove, a Year 1 boy wrote a poem which included the lines:

> Spiderman is good
> I am good
> Spiderman is kind
> I am kind
> I am Spiderman

For this boy, the most significant characteristics of Spider-Man recorded in his poem were not his costume or web or powers, but his *moral identity*. This aspect of Spider-Man seemed to be the source of his appeal to this boy, and it was this aspect of the character that the boy's poem focused on.

The narrative scenarios explored in conflict play can also have a deep appeal, reinforced, to some extent, by their familiarity on television and film. Whatever the source material of the narratives (e.g. *Tommy Zoom, Scooby-Doo, Ben 10, Doctor Who, The Transformers, Spider-Man, Star Wars* or *Warhammer 40,000*) or the materials used to support the resultant play (e.g. toy soldiers and fortresses, make-believe swords, toy 'light-sabres', dressing-up clothes, action figures or manufactured games) the children are likely to be playing out narratives that relate to important themes ranging from protection (such as in all *Captain Scarlet* stories, where the Mysteron threat to humanity needs to be overcome) to the establishment of truth (such as in most *Scooby-Doo* stories, where the ghost or monster is revealed to be someone trying to scare people off for some advantage for himself or herself). All these narratives, along with many others, can be understood to be explorations of two key overarching themes: 'being on the side of good rather than evil' and 'ensuring a good outcome for others' (as will be demonstrated later in this book).

This is where the theory of narrative psychology comes in. This approach to psychology revolves around the notion that humans develop their understanding of the world through the stories that they share. Many modern theorists have explored this idea, the most notable being Jerome Bruner, but the idea itself can be traced back as far as Aristotle (384–322 BC), who considered that desirable human virtues could be best understood by being dramatized in stories that brought them and the consequences of their presence or absence to light. A story would have the capacity to show how a virtue (such as kindness or integrity) could be put into practice and what the impact of this might be, or, conversely, show the effects of withholding such a virtue.

Aristotle's focus was the moral impact of stories (which is a theme that will be returned to later) but many recent writers have suggested that stories might have an even greater effect on our understanding. Inglis (1993: 214) claimed: 'The stories we tell ourselves about ourselves are not just a help to moral education; they comprise the only education which can gain purchase on the modern world.' What this is getting at is the notion that, in order to understand something, we put it into some kind of *narrative construction* in our minds: in other words, we surround the object of our thinking with a plot-line, a series of events, a thematic context and, possibly, other characters. We create a narrative structure and a context for whatever it is we are thinking about. Bruner termed this the 'narrative mode' (Bruner 1986: 13) of thinking, and later argued that: 'One of the principal ways our minds are shaped to daily life is through the stories we tell and listen to – whether truth or fiction. We learn our culture principally through the stories that circulate within its bounds' (Bruner 2006: 230).

For Bruner, we do not just accumulate knowledge, form concepts and come to conclusions in a neutral, logical and scientific manner; we also relate everything we learn and experience to stories that offer exemplars about our condition. An example would be falling in love: we do not just have our own personal experience of falling in love to lead our understanding of the phenomenon, we also have all the stories that we have been exposed to, whether they are *Cinderella*, *Grease*, *Romeo and Juliet*, *Lois & Clark*, *High School Musical*, or the story of our own parents in family photo albums.

Indeed, according to theorists ranging from MacIntyre (1981) to Polkinghorne (1988) and Bruner (1986, 1990, 2006), these narratives form the key *frames of reference* by which we understand our own personal experience. We do not just experience falling in love, we surround our experience with predications and expectations and comparisons, all of which come through the various factual and fictional stories that we have absorbed from birth. We may even form cognitive schemas based around such narratives.

This, of course, applies to the area of human conflict too. We do not just learn about actual human conflict from watching the news and our own experiences, we bring to bear all the real and fictional stories that we know about war, or survival, or enforced loss, or protection, or duty, or victimization, or sacrifice, or peace-making, or compassion, and so on. As adults, we *think* through these types of theme; as children we *play* through them too (see Chapter 5). When children engage in a game that involves representations of guns being wielded, or tanks smashing into each other, or the villain of the piece clutching his chest where he has been shot and rolling to the floor, then they are not simply acting out a kind of wished-for violence that they desire in real life; rather, they are engaged in developmentally appropriate exploration of the types of theme (and all their potential anxieties) noted above, and this exploration is taking the shape of familiar, stimulating and important narratives that are being brought to life through the medium of play.

Eventually, greatly as a result of being exposed to all these stories and playing through possible consequences of events and different endings to the narratives that inform their play, children become adults who are able to explore deep moral issues such as whether, and under what circumstances, war and conflict can ever be just. As a result it could be argued that banning conflict play on the assumption that it automatically promotes real violence might actually remove a potential arena for children's sophisticated exploration and thought about some deep and difficult issues that beset humankind.

2 The argument that superheroes equate to the normalization or glorification of violence

The Early Years Foundation Stage (EYFS) was launched in September 2007, with a revised version published in March 2012. Since September 2008 its status has been statutory, and one of its prime functions is to set out a commonly agreed identification of good practice in the early years. Some care has been taken over its format so it can be used in professional training at different levels, ranging from BTEC to MA. One key feature of the first version of the EYFS was its use of A4-size 'Principles into Practice' cards, which students and professionals could share and discuss during their training. These cards attempted to sum up the key aspects of good practice in the early years that the EYFS was trying to promote, and all the statements that appeared on these cards were chosen with some care.

This makes the appearance of the following statement on one of the cards rather interesting. The theme of 'Principles into Practice' card 4.1 is 'Play and Exploration', and the advice to early years practitioners is that they should: 'Value play which is based on people such as superheroes who may mean a lot to children, *even if you do not appreciate them yourself!*' (Department for Children, Schools and Families (DCSF) 2008a; emphasis added). The first part of the statement, the acknowledgement that early years children might quite like superheroes, is not contentious (though it does, in itself, suggest that there might be some mileage in utilizing this attraction). The second part, however, is more questionable. There is clearly an assumption that, as a group, early years professionals have a low opinion of superheroes. And, of course, the literature on the subject does seem to suggest that the EYFS's statement accurately reflects the common perspective that seems to have been visited upon superheroes in early years circles for many years.

Interestingly, though, there is no such general objection to superheroes in society. The remarkable and sustained success (both financial and critical) of superheroes films such as the *Spider-Man* series (2002–2012), the *X-Men* series (2000 onwards), the recent *Avengers* (2012) and Christian Bale *Batman* films (2005–2012), and the constant production of other well-received superhero films by Hollywood, seems to suggest that society in general is rather taken by superheroes. This is not just evident in the cinema. The television series *Smallville* remained in production between 2000 and 2010, while the *Batman Live World Arena Tour* (Berkowitz et al. 2011–) has generated a great deal of interest and large ticket sales. It does seem, therefore, that superheroes are popular in society at large, and that this popularity seems to be in no danger of dying out just yet.

The rather cautious perspective that early years educators seem to have about superheroes is explained by the prevalent idea (similar to the perspective meted out to war and weapon play) that superheroes equate to the normalization or glorification of violence – in fact, that violence is the central dynamic and theme of superhero figures and narratives. Other aspects that superhero characters or stories might contain seem overlooked or at least remain minor or unimportant to many early years professionals and other child educators writing in the field.

Examples of this understanding of superheroes are easy to come by. Brodkin's article, 'When superheroes invade' (2003), is a typical case in point, and illustrates the type of professional hesitation that exists. Brodkin (2003: 38) starts by describing the ideal situation that many teachers and early years professionals wish to achieve:

> YOUR CLASSROOM
> Many children are completely at ease with the opportunity to play out their feelings and fantasies. Their play is rich with language opportunities, wonderfully interactive and cognitively complex.

This idyllic picture of a classroom, however, is soon under threat. Brodkin (2003: 38) continues:

> But for some, that play draws heavily on contemporary media fare, especially television programming. Result – the ubiquitous 'superheroes' invade your classroom and bring aggressive themes (perhaps bordering on violence) too close to comfort. What do you do? First, don't be shocked.

A quick review of the language and structure of this argument illustrates the type of concern that Brodkin has identified: superheroes are by nature 'aggressive', bordering on violent; they are 'ubiquitous' (like some kind of ever-present nuisance to deal with); they 'invade' one's classroom (a telling word that suggests that superheroes have no natural home there); they reduce the quality of the play and need some kind of rejecting adult response. The final suggestion that the disruption caused by superhero play is enough to cause 'shock' serves to indicate that superhero play is frequently found to be relentlessly destructive.

Other examples from the literature tell a similar story. The title of Bauer and Dettore's (1997) article, 'Superhero play: What's a teacher to do?', conjures up visions of hapless teachers helplessly shrugging their shoulders while their errant children embark upon unwanted superhero play before their eyes, while Holland's article, 'Just pretending', describes superhero play as one of various possible 'aggressive elements of dramatic play' (Holland 1999: 1). Dixon's *Playing Them False* (1990) considers play based around some then-contemporary superheroes (such as He-Man) as well as more well-established ones such as Spider-Man, and feels that a 'power-crazed and macho atmosphere' (Dixon 1990: 134) is predominant in such play. Levin and Carlsson-Paige (2006: 16) also point the finger squarely at superheroes for being responsible for promoting violence while referring to films starring various characters including Spider-Man and the Hulk: 'It is these violent media and the accompanying merchandising campaigns that draw young children into a culture of violence.'

This, in a nutshell, is the common perspective and fear of many teachers and early years professionals; for them, all superheroes do is put a colourful, child-friendly gloss on violence, and they and the violent culture that they represent so attractively are to be rejected as dangerous.

Response: Superhero narratives have an overriding concern with questions of moral responsibility

The possible problem with this view of superheroes, as recognized by many authors writing in different fields (such as theology and philosophy), is that the key dynamic of superheroes is not violence, even though violence is often used as part of the narrative structure and conventional style of most superhero stories. The key dynamic, rather, is the theme of *moral responsibility*, which plays out in four major ways:

(a) investigating the possible nature of goodness;
(b) determining what it is to be a good person, and why it is important to be one;
(c) exploring good's struggle to overcome evil while maintaining its integrity;
(d) communicating the importance of recognizing and living up to one's moral responsibility.

Much of this book will be devoted to an exploration of how children's engagement with superheroes can draw out these themes and impact upon children's moral growth as a result, but a few examples drawn from superhero narratives aimed at a variety of age groups will suffice to demonstrate the point.

Example 1: The Numberjacks

The Numberjacks (2007 onwards) are, essentially, animated numerals from 0 to 9. Their storylines (which are aimed at an audience aged mainly between 3 and 5) involve resolving a variety of mathematical problems to do with number, shape, size, pattern, and so on, all with the help of human child 'agents' who contact them to give guidance that will aid them in their tasks. They are marketed as 'superhero numbers battling with Meanies and solving problems in the real world' (Open Mind Productions 2007: 2).

As with all well-developed superheroes, the Numberjacks have their opposing supervillains; these being the Numbertaker, the Shape-Japer, the Problem-Blob and Spooky Spoon (who mixes thing up). There is even a supervillain who seems highly inspired by *Batman*'s 'the Riddler', called 'the Puzzler', whose modus operandi is virtually the same, and who even wears Riddler-like green goggles.

There is absolutely no violence in the stories at all: instead, the main dynamic is that one of the supervillains will cause a problem, such as clothes becoming the wrong length, or things turning upside-down, or a boy having all the food on his plate while the girl next to him has none. Once the Numberjacks identify the pattern in what has gone wrong, everything goes back to normal and the supervillain of the story disappears into the distance.

All this may seem very trivial, except for two things. The Numberjacks are not just faced with a mathematical predicament in each of their stories, they are also faced with a traditional *moral* problem: that of the need to respect and, if need be, restore the *natural order* of things. In all *Numberjack* stories, the restoration of the proper state of things is the desired and successful result. The integrity of the world needs to be protected.

This emphasis on the need to respect, sustain and ensure the natural order of things has been a key concern in moral thinking at least since Aristotle (384–322 BC), who considered that what he determined to be the human 'virtues' (including moral virtues and the exercise of reason) were to be considered as virtues precisely because they exemplified human beings operating in their *proper, natural state*. In other words, we are at our best and most perfectly realized when we conform to the natural order. The same idea later found expression in the works of St. Thomas Aquinas (1225–1274), who believed that all human beings should follow moral laws which, for him, were exemplified in nature and originated and constituted by God. This 'natural law' theory suggested that the universe was governed by 'laws considered "natural" in the sense of being derived from nature and therefore seen as providing universal moral standards that are binding' (Stokes 2003: 214).

The second thing to note about all *Numberjacks* narratives is that the viewer is actively encouraged to consider *consequences*. In every story Numberjack 5 says, 'But if everything [mentions the problem] then *anything* might happen!', and then imagines (with the aid of cartoon drawings) all the undesirable situations that would beset the world if that story's problem is allowed to remain unresolved.

There are two observations to make on this. First of all, as discussed by Piaget (1932/1965) and Kohlberg (1984), the child's developing ability to consider consequences is central to his or her eventual development of substantial moral principles and understanding (see Chapter 4). Secondly, many of the gentle situations posited by the *Numberjacks* stories can be understood as embryonic starting points for the child's eventual engagement with the deepest moral issues.

Let us consider the problem set in the *Numberjacks* story, *A Record in the Charts* (2009), for example. The situation is that the girl has no food on her plate while the boy has twice as much food as he needs. This is not just a mathematical problem, for if we follow Numberjack 5's train of thought and consider what might happen if this situation is left to continue in the long run, we might eventually find ourselves dealing with deep issues of famine and inequality. Similarly, we could start off by exploring the gentle *Numberjacks* narratives that centre around the restoration of the proper and desirable order of things, but (if we explore this issue through to its logical conclusion) we might end up with *Macbeth*.

Example 2: Dialogues between Batman and Superman

Children's engagement with Batman and Superman individually will be explored later in this book, but one of the most productive by-products of their both being owned by the same publishing company (DC Comics) is the dialogue between them that has been developed since the 1940s. Two samples of this ongoing dialogue will suffice to demonstrate how superheroes (when written at their best) deal with deep moral issues.

World's Finest Comics was a vehicle for stories that featured both Batman and Superman together. Issue no. 222 (April 1974) of this comic featured an 'imaginary' story set sometime in the near future, when Batman and Superman are raising their sons as the next generation of heroes. The opening full-page panel of the story (written by Bob Haney and illustrated by Dick Dillin and Vince Colletta) features the elder Batman and Superman giving moral instruction to their sons:

> Batman: Hear me, Son! Man is *evil*! Only law and order can stand between us and our own savage, criminal natures! An eye for an eye . . . a tooth for a tooth . . . *that's* the only way civilization can survive!
> Superman: Don't ever forget, Son – Man is basically *good*! He may do bad things at times . . . but, in the end, his good nature must triumph!
>
> (Haney et al. 1974: 1)

The story itself concerns two parallel research projects, each of which attempts to find out which of these two discourses about human nature is right. Batman Junior and Superman Junior find themselves on different sides of the argument to begin with, and the story charts how their opinions on the (enormously profound) issue evolve.

(Anecdotally, I know of at least four children who read this story when it came out and found themselves inspired to consider deep philosophical ideas about the moral character of humanity. Two are now priests, one does substantial voluntary work for her synagogue and one worked as a nursery and primary school teacher before becoming a university lecturer (me). All have worked, and continue to work, towards the moral education of children.)

The second sample of dialogue comes from another, more recent, 'imaginary' story, *Kingdom Come* by Mark Waid and Alex Ross (2008), which features Superman and Batman in their sixties coming out of retirement to deal with the prevalent issue of the day (which is that of a new phenomenon of superpowered people acting without any of the level of moral responsibility or restraint that either character approves of, and threatening to overpower all 'normal' human beings). This comic-book narrative (like most superhero narratives currently published in comic books rather than in other media) is aimed at older teen and young adult readers. In one section of the story, Superman tries to convince Batman of his view of what is really at stake:

> Batman: Did you ever *consider* that a *war* might be for the *best*? That perhaps humanity's *only chance* is for the superhumans to swallow *each other*?
>
> Superman: Don't give me that! The deliberate taking of human – even *super*-human – life goes against every belief I *have* – *and* that *you* have. That's the *one thing* we've *always* had in *common*. It's what *made* us what we *are*. More than anyone else in the world, when you scratch everything else away from *Batman*, you're left with someone who *doesn't want to see anybody die.*

(Waid and Ross 2008: 151)

The entire narrative of *Kingdom Come* is centred around the issues of the relationship between power and moral responsibility, what methods good is justified (or not justified) in using in attempting to defeat evil, and what happens to one's character as a result of the choices one makes in response to these issues. This seems to be far removed from any simple glorification or promotion of violence.

Example 3: The origin of Spider-Man

Spider-Man's origin story (1962 – recently retold in the 2012 film *The Amazing Spider-Man*) illustrates how important the theme of moral responsibility is in superhero narratives. In this story we meet Peter Parker, who is skinny, bespectacled and picked on by his classmates at college. The only people who seem to care for him are his Aunt May and Uncle Ben, who are bringing him up like their own son. Once Peter gains his 'spider-powers' (through the bite of a radioactive spider), his first thought is that he could use his new powers to make some money.

This hardly seems heroic so far, but Spider-Man is being set up by his author Stan Lee to learn a harsh moral lesson. While earning money from showing off his spider-powers, Spider-Man allows a thief to run past him and escape. The policeman chasing the criminal castigates Spider-Man for letting the thief go, but Spider-Man replies that it is nothing to do with him. This does not remain the case, however, as Peter travels home, only to find that his beloved Uncle Ben has been shot dead by the criminal that he had let escape earlier. 'My fault! – All my fault!' sobs Peter, before Stan Lee, the author and narrator of this, the very first Spider-Man story ever published, concludes: 'And a lean, silent figure fades slowly into the gathering darkness, aware at last that in this world with great power must also come great responsibility!' (Lee and Ditko 1962: 11). Spider-Man has learnt the hard way that power must be used wisely and for the good of others, or unwanted consequences can result. He is wracked with guilt, and this informs all his classic stories.

Layman (2005: 195) suggests that Spider-Man's origin story, and its culmination in this realization, is actually an exploration of

> one of the all-time classic philosophical questions, 'Why be moral?' The traditional superhero is, after all, committed to promoting good and fighting evil. He is dedicated to seeing justice prevail over injustice, and this is the core concern of morality as a whole.

Layman sees superheroes engaged in an approach to morality that centres around the importance of *justice*. This 'justice' approach to morality derives from Lawrence Kohlberg (1984), who argued that the pursuit of justice for all (so, *fairness* and fair treatment) was the key task of morality, and that developed moral reasoning involved the ability to define and apply key moral principles in the service of such justice. This approach to morality can certainly be seen in the great majority of superhero narratives, where the plot dynamics typically involve the defeat of such threats to justice as theft, blackmail, corruption, terrorism, the menacing of the community and imminent death, and where the superhero characters themselves operate in accordance with their own well-defined ethical principles (e.g. that of preserving life shared by Superman and Batman).

What can be forgotten, however, is that superhero characters and narratives also centrally concern themselves with what has been described as a morality of *care*. This approach to morality was identified by Carol Gilligan (1982: 19) who argued that: 'This conception of morality as concerned with the activity of care centres moral development around the understanding of responsibility and relationships, just as the conception of morality as fairness ties moral development to the understanding of rights and rules.'

Such an approach to morality can be seen in virtually all superhero stories since Superman first rescued Lois Lane and Batman rescued the young boy Dick Grayson, both in 1939. A more recent example, from an episode of *Batman: The Animated Series* shown on television in the early 1990s, demonstrates this very well.

Example 4: 'Cat Scratch Fever'

The plot of this episode ('Cat Scratch Fever': Derek and Dixon 1992) concerns unethical businessman Roland Daggett's attempts to unleash a plague of rabies on Gotham City before then selling the city at a highly inflated price his own manufactured antidote to the very disease that he has inflicted on the population. (More will be said about this modern type of supervillain in Chapter 8.) The emotional centre of the story, however, concerns Selina (Catwoman) Kyle's grief for the loss of her beloved cat, Isis.

Isis is captured by two of Daggett's goons near the beginning of the story, and Catwoman embarks on a futile quest to search him down and rescue him. Throughout the story we see her gaze despondently at photographs of Isis and become close to tears. Right at the end of the episode, however, just as Selina is about to give up all hope, we see a basket lowered through the open window behind her. As Selina picks up her photograph of Isis one more time we see her beloved cat emerge from the basket and meow in her ear. Selina is so overcome with joy that she hugs Isis tightly and literally dances with joy, a tear falling down her cheek. Then she crosses to the open window, where she sees Batman swinging off into the distance as the story ends.

The point is that Batman did not *have* to try to find and rescue Isis in order to defeat Daggett, but, out of care and compassion for Selina Kyle, he did so anyway. What the 5–12-year-old viewer understands from this is that Batman cares for her, that he performs actions to express this care, that he has reunited two beings who love each other and had been cruelly separated, and that, because of all these things, he is a good man.

The centrality of superheroes' concern with questions about morality and being of good moral character is further illustrated through *Spider-Man, Spider-Man 2* and *Spider-Man 3* film director Sam Raimi's comments to *Screentalk* magazine about filming such a person:

> Any story of a hero shows us the good that we are capable of – [that's] the value of these types of tales. I knew . . . that millions of kids would come see this movie, I just knew it, and they would look up to

> Spider-man . . . Therefore I felt it was very important that I put a morally responsible character up there. Someone that would be worthy of that admiration . . . Someone who went from somewhat selfish to someone who used their abilities to help others. It's more than beating up the bad guys.
>
> (O'Hara 2002: 41)

All superheroes perpetually wrestle with issues of moral responsibility and, to use an old-fashioned term, noble behaviour, and it can be argued that these things drive and sustain superhero narratives more than the dynamic of violence. As Kaveney (2008: 4) observes:

> A superhero is a man or woman with powers that are either massive extensions of human strengths and capabilities, or fundamentally different in kind, which she or he uses to fight for truth, justice and the protection of the innocent.

This might suggest that there is some scope in using superheroes with children as resources in their moral education, and that the understandable caution that many teachers and early years professionals seem to have towards superheroes might be alleviated by such use. Later chapters of this book will discuss some possibilities in this area in more detail.

3 The argument that superheroes offer up negative, stereotypical and destructive role models of masculinity and femininity

It has long been observed that it is mainly (if not exclusively) boys who are interested in superheroes and conflict play – see Parsons (1991), Fingeroth (2004) and Kaveney (2008), for example. It can also be observed that reservations about superheroes and conflict play mainly stem from female authors – such as Holland (1999), Marsh (2000), Brodkin (2003) and Levin and Carlsson-Paige (2006), to name but a few. This dichotomy deserves some exploration, but it might, to some extent, represent what can be seen as an increasing 'feminization' of primary education and the accompanying mainly female attempts to explain and deal with what are regarded as rather alien and unvalued male preoccupations and behaviour. These attempts manifest themselves in several forms, all of which deserve some explanation, but the important point is that many of them find expression in what can be understood as some kind of negation or rejection of boys' interests and play.

The authors who try to account for the 'maleness' of boys' engagement with superheroes and conflict play soon find themselves needing to account for the 'maleness' (and, indeed, 'femaleness') of *any* type of behaviour or interest – in other words, they try to explain why boys and girls seem to behave and think differently from each other in the first place. It comes as no surprise that the two main types of explanation offered (see Lippa 2005) are those that suggest that boys and girls think and behave the way that they do because of natural, biological differences, and those that suggest that maleness and femaleness (or 'masculinity' and 'femininity' – the terms adopted tend to represent any particular author's stance on the matter) are essentially socially learnt or culturally constructed behaviours and thought-patterns (see Thorne 1993).

It is the second of these types of explanation that presently dominates commentary about primary education, often in the context of discussions about what seems to be a current phenomenon of boys' educational under-achievement. For example, according to Skelton and Francis (2003: 6): 'Feminist researchers have tended to see boys' underachievement in particular subjects as due to their constructions of gender, and indeed due to the dominant constructions of desirable masculinity in society at large.' What this is really alluding to is the notion that boys do not do as well as girls in school because the character and behavioural traits associated with masculinity are actually quite destructive, anti-social and anti-educational. For such authors – see MacNaughton (2000), Connell (2005) and Warrington and Younger (2006), for example – the culture that surrounds children contains and promotes ideas about masculinity that work against children's best interests: for example, that being non-conformist, or confrontational, or aggressive or having the potential for violence are 'proper' masculine characteristics; while studying, or conforming to authority figures' requirements, or reading, or expressing emotion, or even achieving academically are behaviours exhibited by those whose masculinity is weak or in question.

It can be suggested that there might be a relationship between this kind of opinion about ideas about masculinity and a negative regard for superheroes and conflict play, as these could be perceived as things that idealize and promote such ideas about masculinity. As discussed earlier, superhero and conflict play is often judged by what is understood to be its propensity for promoting confrontational behaviour and violence, and, as a consequence, is rejected by many teachers and educators. Now, however, there might be an additional dimension to this rejection. If disapproval exists, then what might be being disapproved of is not just a form of play, but any questionable 'dominant constructions of desirable masculinity in society at large' (Skelton and Francis 2003: 6) that might be perceived as being part of superhero culture. These constructions might be rejected because they are deemed to be (a) destructive, and (b) artificially imposed and promoted by the dominant group in society (i.e. men) as part of a means to retain their dominance (see MacNaughton 2000).

When it comes to superhero and conflict play, the attempt to challenge these presupposed 'dominant constructions of masculinity' (Francis and Skelton 2003: 6) and the perceived domination of men over women takes several forms. The first of these is the banning approach, identified by Holland (2003) and discussed earlier. The second approach is in favour of 'de-gendering' boys' and girls' play completely by removing any type of play or play resource deemed as gender-specific (Thompson 2009), which might include superhero and conflict play if these are regarded as specifically male-orientated.

There is a third approach, too. This approach acknowledges that girls can be interested in superhero and conflict play as well as boys, but it also sees the predominance of boys involved in such play as a potential obstacle for girls who wish to join in – as aptly illustrated by the title of Marsh's article, '"But I w⌐ ᵗ to fly too!": Girls and Superhero Play in the Infant Classroom' (2000). ˥mbination of what are regarded as poor constructions of masculinity ˙s' domination of superhero and conflict play is perceived by Marsh as ˧ most unhelpful to girls.

Also documented is a feeling that it is not just superhero culture's constructions of masculinity that are dubious and unhelpful, but its constructions of femininity too. For example, in the article just referred to, Marsh (2000: 211) states:

> The male superhero figures live in a world where women are either wholly evil or wholly good . . . the good girls simper and whimper and, if they are pretty enough, receive romantic attention from the heroes. The evil women . . . are usually portrayed as desexualised, physically unattractive characters. Female heroes . . . are not as brave and strong as the boys.

One can see how any educators or early years professionals who hold this perspective about superheroes would think twice about the wisdom of allowing or engaging with them in the classroom. However, I would argue that many other more positive and complex representations of femininity can also be found too, as will now be demonstrated.

Response: Superheroes can offer up very positive role models for both boys and girls, and children's natural play and interests can be respected and allowed

There are two significant types of female character in superhero narratives: those with superpowers and those without. Both deserve some exploration.

The key female superhero to discuss is also the very first, namely Wonder Woman. This character made her first appearance in January 1942, and was created by Dr. William Moulton Marston (a classically educated Harvard psychologist) precisely to be a strong female role model and archetype and a corrective to what he saw at the time as:

> blood-curdling masculinity . . . it's smart to be strong; it's big to be generous, but it's sissified, according to exclusively male rules, to be tender, loving, affectionate and alluring . . . not even girls want to be girls as long as our feminine archetype lacks force, strength and power. Not wanting to be girls, they don't want to be tender . . . peace-loving as good women are. Women's strong qualities have been despised because of their weakness. The obvious remedy is to create a feminine character with all the strength of Superman plus all the allure of a good and beautiful woman.
>
> (Marston 1943, quoted in Robbins 1996: 18)

Wonder Woman was just such a character. She was an Amazon princess who lived with her mother Queen Hippolyte and the other Amazons from Greek mythology on the women-only Paradise Island and counted the goddesses Athena and Aphrodite among her friends and comrades. Her engagement with the rest of the world starts when she rescues the pilot Steve Trevor, who has crash-landed on the island, and who then convinces her to go to America with him to help in the fight against the Nazis, whose values are anathema to her. The historical timing of her arrival was, perhaps, not accidental:

> All of a sudden women were abandoning traditional roles and you had 'Rosie the Riveter' and you had women building aircraft carriers. All of a sudden it made sense to have a female superhero who could stand toe-to-toe with Superman and Batman.
>
> (Gregory Noveck in Gray and Maynard 2008)

Wonder Woman remains in America after the war to fight whatever causes are contemporary with the creation of her stories.

It is worth noting that almost her first act is one of traditional role-reversal: we see a woman rescuing a man – and an active, fit member of the armed forces at that. From then on part of Wonder Woman's role was to comment on what she saw as particularly male views of and approaches to the world. She acts as a voice of conscience, but also a figure of power who does not need men to sort things out for her. Kaveney (2008: 18) describes her as one of the two 'strongest and most active women in popular media. Wonder Woman was so obviously a feminist icon that she was condemned by Wertham [a psychologist of the time who also condemned Batman] as a possible lesbian role-model.'

Wonder Woman continues to be a strong, powerful, thoughtful, intelligent and beautiful woman who makes a difference: in *Kingdom Come* (Waid and Ross 2008), it is Wonder Woman who rescues Superman from despair and gives him a sense of purpose and a reason to be hopeful for the future. The bestselling author Jodi Picoult, who was commissioned by DC Comics to write *Wonder Woman: Love and Murder* (2007), said in her introduction to the story:

> When I seriously began to think of Wonder Woman and my own impressions of her, I knew what I'd have to do: create a storyline that captured her wide demographic of fans – from young women looking for a role model to adults who had grown up with her, male and female – and create a richness and depth of character . . . [There are] universal battles, and it seemed to me that Wonder Woman was plenty strong enough to undertake them.
>
> (Picoult 2007: 5)

The other strong and active superhero story character referred to by Kaveney (2008) is, of course, Lois Lane, the archetype for all non-superpowered female characters in superhero narratives. The whole point of Lois Lane is that she is capable, clever, determined, resourceful, resilient, brave, proud and confident – which is why Superman falls for her in the first place and why she is able to tease Clark Kent, whom she deems as less capable and more timid than herself. Noel Neill, who played Lois Lane in the 1950s *Superman* television series, has talked about the constant stream of letters that she received from women about how much they appreciated the strong, independent, successful-in-her-career role model being offered by her character, and all the actresses who have played Lois Lane attest to these and other admirable qualities, as demonstrated by this statement by Dana Delany, who played her in *Superman – The Animated Adventures*:

> I think that Lois was ahead of her time. After the 'fifties and World War Two we went back to that perfect homemaker – but Lois wasn't that, and I think it was really important to have that as a role-model for girls of my age . . . very fast-paced, no-nonsense, she's got a sharp tongue . . . Lois thinks she can take care of herself and doesn't need anybody.
>
> (DC Comics 2005)

This is typical of female characters in superhero narratives, particularly those from the 1960s onwards. Several commentators, such as Daniels (1991) and Ryall and Tipton (2005), draw attention, for example, to the fact that it is actually Sue (Invisible Woman) Richards (who first appeared in 1961) who steers and determines the fate of the Fantastic Four rather than her husband Reed (the erstwhile leader of the FF), and that she does this through her own consistent courage, strength, determination, sense of vision and commitment to the family group that the FF team is made up of. The Invisible Woman, like Wonder Woman before her and many after, such as Elektra, Ms. Marvel, the Scarlet Witch, Batwoman, and Storm, Rogue, Emma Frost and Jean Grey (of the X-Men – see Chapter 11), typify the strength and resolution of female superheroes, just as Mary Jane Watson, Gwen Stacey, Alicia and others typify that of non-superpowered women in superhero narratives.

As a final note: any reader of superheroes familiar with the Enchantress or Medusa or, indeed, almost any superhero film or comic will know that it is typical for any evil female character to be beguilingly beautiful and tempting rather than desexualized or physically unattractive – see Julie Newmar's Catwoman's persistent attempts to seduce Adam West's Batman throughout the 1960s television series of the same name, for example. It does seem, therefore, that female superheroes are very rarely weaker or less courageous than male superheroes, and they have their own moral attractions: for example, Madrid (2009: v) comments:

> The female superheroes struck me as being more interested in making the world a better place . . . I suppose I was drawn to their compassionate natures . . . To me the superheroines were as beautiful and alluring as the movie stars or the models I saw in my sister's Vogue magazines, but with a bonus – these women were powerful like men.

(Male superheroes are not simple, macho stereotypes either, as was demonstrated a little in Chapter 2 and will continue to be demonstrated in the chapters that follow.)

An even deeper issue

All of this still leaves a possible problem with the 'socially learnt/culturally constructed' explanation of girls' and boys' behaviour patterns. This is that it is a matter of some disagreement whether it is possible to label *any* human behaviours as being identifiable as essentially 'masculine' or 'feminine', except those explicitly connected to biological functions or physiological make-up. For example, it could be argued that being aggressive or violent (for example) is not to be understood just as 'masculine' behaviour, or that being caring or sympathetic (for example) is not to be understood just as 'feminine' behaviour; rather, that all of these are *human* behaviours and attitudes, available to all human beings, regardless of whether they are male or female. As Pinker (1998: 49) states: 'A universal structure to the mind is not only logically possible but likely to be true . . . We must be qualitatively alike.' In other words, *all* human beings, regardless of their perceived masculinity or femininity, have the capacity to be cruel or kind, caring or uncaring, principled or unprincipled, confrontational or non-confrontational, violent or non-violent, and so on – which is one reason, of course, why all significant educational writers from Plato to the present day have put such a high emphasis on the *moral education* of children.

Some possible limitations of the 'socially learnt/culturally constructed' explanation can also be seen by considering the other main rationalization offered for differences between boys and girls, which is that any such differences are predominantly due to natural, biological physiology and function – that is, they are *biologically*, rather than culturally, determined. Many authors, such as Gurian (2002), Gurian and Stevens (2007), Baron-Cohen (2004), James (2007) and Sax (2009), draw attention to significant innate differences between boys and girls and their probable effects. These differences include things such as the obvious physical traits, the development of different parts of the brain and their effects on things such as language development and visual-spatial ability, and hormones such as oestrogen and testosterone and their effects on behaviour. The common conclusion of such authors is, as Gurian (2002: 17) puts it, that differences between boys and girls and men and women originate 'in the brain, with culture playing an important part, but not the defining role that many people have wished to believe'.

In other words, this counter-argument suggests, as Ridley (2004: 55) puts it, that:

> The burden of proof [is] on those who would see a cultural habit rather than an instinct . . . Nurture is reinforcing nature, not opposing it . . . When you see a man chasing a woman just because she is pretty, or a girl playing with a doll while her brother plays with a sword, you can never be sure that what you are seeing is just cultural, because it might have an element of instinct . . . There might be all sorts of cultural aspects to a behaviour that is grounded in instinct. Culture will often reflect human nature rather than affect it.

So perhaps, in the end, superhero characters and narratives are much less two-dimensional than is sometimes supposed, and male and female superheroes alike cannot be so easily understood as offering up any simple role models of masculinity or femininity for boys or girls to emulate, whether one approves of them or not. The following chapters will seek to go beyond such generalizations to see what else might be significant.

This chapter began by observing that it is boys who seem to engage with superhero and conflict play the most. It could be suggested, therefore, that any attempt to edit, 'correct' or veto such play for whatever reason might be mostly felt by boys, and could possibly be understood by them as a rejection or negation of their interests (and, therefore, of themselves). This situation could become even more acute when one remembers that it was recently found that only 13 per cent of all primary school teachers are male (General Teaching Council 2008). Boys, then, not only might regard their desired play and interests as being rejected in school, but also might lack school-based adult male role models who could offer a shared and genuine enthusiasm, understanding and acceptance of what boys find appealing and engaging in superhero narratives and conflict play. This book only deals with one small aspect of children's cultural world, but, even so, the situation of boys potentially ending up feeling left out or rejected even with regard to something that might seem trivial (like superheroes) could be questionable, especially in a climate where boys' underachievement and diminishing engagement with school are real issues.

PART II
Rethinking superhero and conflict play

4 Theoretical understandings of children's moral development

Introduction

One of the key characteristics of being human, and possibly something that separates us from all other creatures, is our capacity for being *moral agents*; in other words, being capable of making and reflecting upon moral decisions, principles and behaviour. Our contemplation of morality and what it is to be moral might, in fact, be central to our humanity. One of the greatest philosophers of all, Immanuel Kant (1724–1804) considered that there was a universal demand on all human beings to be as morally good as they could be at all times, something that he termed a 'categorical imperative' (Kant 1983: 84). For Kant, part of the task of being human was to seek to determine the most proper moral behaviour in any given situation one might find oneself in.

A key way of doing this would be to consider a possible course of action and ask oneself what the consequences would be if everyone acted in that fashion. For example, what if a man looked in a shop window and passionately desired an object that he could not afford? Should he just take it anyway because of his deep wish to have it? But what would happen if everybody acted in such a manner? A few moments of rational deliberation would probably be enough for this man to realize that the consequences of such a situation would be highly undesirable. Therefore, since it would not be desirable for everyone to steal things that did not belong to them, the man should not do it either. As Reed (2000: 320) puts it: 'Everyone knows that societies would fall apart if their members adopted maxims which urged murder, adultery, stealing, lying, envy and seeking to deprive others of what they have, dishonour of parents, etc.' In other words, people should adopt the moral principles and behaviour that they would wish everyone else to adopt too. This is what Kant termed 'a universal law' (Kant 1983: 86) of morality, something that is available to everyone through the power of reason.

The question emerges, then, how children become capable of such reasoning about morality, and how they develop into moral agents capable of rational and emotional reflection about moral decisions, principles, behaviour and consequences. This chapter explores some of the major ideas about children's moral development that have been put forward in recent times to see if any possible answers to this question emerge.

A 'morality of justice' and a 'morality of care'

A good starting place is an acknowledgement of two key types of morality to have been identified and investigated: a 'morality of justice' and a 'morality of care'. Both approaches to morality are compatible with each other, though each emphasizes different things.

The 'justice' approach to morality can be seen in the work of Jean Piaget (1932/1965) and, particularly, Lawrence Kohlberg (1984). Kohlberg argued that the pursuit of justice for all (in other words, fairness, fair treatment and equality) was the key task of morality, and that this task involved the capability to define and apply key moral *principles* as fairly as possible in the service of justice. For Kohlberg (and Piaget before him) such ability rested upon sophisticated moral *reasoning* (just as it did for Kant), and so the emphasis of research into the formation of children's 'morality of justice' has been on their developing *cognitive* abilities.

The 'care' approach to morality can be seen most prominently in the work of Carol Gilligan (1982). She argued that moral decisions, responses and choices of behaviour were not just borne out of rationality and a consideration of the moral principles that could possibly apply, but owed themselves much more to a sense of responsibility to others. For Gilligan, moral behaviour rested upon *compassion* for one's fellow creatures and the human impulse to care for them and nurture their well-being. In any scenario, the decision about which course of action to pursue might prioritize the well-being of the *people* involved over the possible moral principles that might apply. (An example might be of a woman who has committed a crime of theft which, if the moral principle that it is wrong to steal was followed through, might lead to her imprisonment, but the decision is taken not to imprison her – even though she deserves it – because of the detrimental effect this could have on the well-being of her young baby.) The emphasis of research into the formation of children's 'morality of care', then, has often been on their *emotional and social* development and behaviour towards others.

Interestingly, one of Gilligan's strong suggestions was that a gender divide existed here: that it was predominantly boys and men who developed a morality of justice (i.e. they were more concerned with the application of moral principles and the pursuit of fair outcomes) and girls and women who developed a morality of care (i.e. they were more concerned with the well-being of individual people and the pursuit of nurturing outcomes). This suggestion has not been borne out by subsequent research; the current consensus of opinion (see Jorgensen 2006, for example) is that both types of morality exist alongside each other and inform each other, but girls and boys are equally capable and orientated to develop both a morality of justice *and* a morality of care.

Children's development of moral values and behaviour

According to the great majority of researchers in the field, children's development of these two types of morality seems to occur in stages. Piaget, the first key figure to explore children's moral development, considered that the nature of children's moral thinking depended on their ability to *decentre* – to understand that other people have their own views of the world and that these views might well be different from the child's. Until children developed such an understanding securely (which, for Piaget, was around the age of 6 or 7), then they would not be able to empathize with others. This would mean that children at this young age would not be able to take into account people's motives or intentions when judging any example of their behaviour, and would only be interested in the effects of this behaviour. Piaget termed this focus on consequences only *moral realism* (Piaget 1932/1965: 104), and considered that moral realism was the first stage of children's moral development.

Children's responses to and understanding of rules are also a key signifier of their stage of morality. Children in the stage of moral realism, according to Piaget, regard rules as fixed and permanent. The nature of the rules in children's lives depends on what the adults around them expose them to (e.g. the rules might be anything from being quiet while Mummy is on the telephone to following the Ten Commandments) but, as suggested by Turiel (2002), they can be seen as falling into three categories: rules that are explicitly to do with *morals*, such as not hurting other children deliberately; rules that are to do with *social conventions*, such as wearing school uniform to go to school; and rules that are to do with *personal conduct*, such as washing one's hands after going to the toilet.

All these norms and rules are set by authorities such as parents, teachers and the law. The child in the 'moral realism' stage regards such norms and rules as inviolable, and considers that punishment is due if they are transgressed. Most importantly, for Piaget, 'neither logical nor moral norms are innate in the individual mind' (Piaget 1932/1965: 405); in other words, children in this stage of moral development do not really have ownership of their moral views, rules, values or principles, as all these things have been generated and authorized by the outside world.

Significantly, moral norms and rules are not just set through explicit instructions and lists of desirable and undesirable behaviour (such as the lists of 'class rules' typically seen in most reception and primary classrooms), but also through the real-life behaviour modelled by authority figures such as teachers and parents and, as children get older, others in their peer groups too. The famous 'Bobo doll' experiment (Bandura et al. 1961, 1963) involved children aged 3–5 observing an adult through a one-way window as she interacted with various toys, one of which was a giant doll weighted at its bottom end so it would always return to its original upright position if knocked down. The children watched the woman be very violent towards the Bobo doll, both verbally and physically, before leaving the room. When the children later entered the room containing the Bobo doll, they imitated the woman's aggressive behaviour towards it, except if they had also seen the woman seemingly receive punishment for her actions (which happened in some of the versions of the experiment); in this case they did not reproduce her violent behaviour. This experiment set the tone for what has become known as *social learning theory*. As Van Evra (2004: 4) puts it: 'Individuals are more likely to perform modelled actions that are valued rather than those acts that are not rewarded or punished.'

This is one of the main reasons why the educational community, from the early years upwards, has adopted positive reinforcement as a key behavioural management strategy: the notion is that if children witness not just desirable behaviour but desirable behaviour being rewarded and praised, then they will be more likely to adopt such behaviour for themselves. It is also a key reason why so much emphasis is put on the importance of teachers and early years professionals being *good role models*; for example, the 2008 version of the Practice Guidance for the EYFS states that 'children need adults to set a good example' (DCSF 2008a: 24). (The importance of good role models – and, in particular, the potential that *superheroes* have for being such things – will be discussed further in Chapter 7.)

Another key aspect of social learning theory is the notion that children develop what Bruner (1990: 48) termed 'situational schemas'. A schema, according to Athey (1990: 26), is 'a pattern of repeatable behaviour into which experiences are assimilated and that are gradually co-ordinated'. A situational schema, therefore, is a pattern of behaviour repeatedly observed, repeatedly practised and cognitively related to a particular social context, such as washing one's hands before a meal or looking both ways before crossing the road. Bruner's (1990: 48) own lovely example was that 'When people go into the post-office, they behave "post-office"'.

Situational schemas reflect moral values and principles too; for example, the situational schema of regularly tidying up after oneself before playtime reflects the moral principle of fairness in that it is fair to take responsibility for one's own mess and unfair to expect anyone else to have to do so for you. The important thing here is that children seem to absorb and imitate the behaviour that they see valued, modelled and promoted in the first instance (certainly during the stage of moral realism); and then, as their cognitive abilities and reasoning develop (see below), children become able to take increasing control over their own choices of behaviour and their reasons for these choices.

As children's ability to decentre grows, they become increasingly interested in the motives and reasons that might lie behind any type of behaviour, and these things take on more and more importance in their moral thinking. Children now begin to move away from moral realism towards what Piaget (1932/1965: 355) termed 'moral autonomy'. This stage of moral development is marked by children's capacity to consider both the motives and reasons that inform choices of behaviour as well as the outcomes of these choices, and the development of the children's own self-identified moral standards and principles. Children in this stage can take rules, laws, values and principles that they originally received from authorities in the outside world, and check for themselves whether these things are valid or not. If the children agree that any of these values or principles are valid, they now determine for themselves how they might best be applied and what types of behaviour might best match them. If the children consider that any received values, rules and principles are not valid after all, they then determine what they might be replaced with. In other words, children in this stage develop proper ownership over their own moral values, principles, rules and behaviour.

Let us look at an example of this in practice. As part of my own research a range of children of different ages in one West Sussex school were invited to respond to several questions about their own moral values and ideas about being good. The responses to the question 'What makes a good person? Please explain' were very consistent over different age ranges, with both younger children (Years 2 and 3) and older children (Years 4 and 5) offering statements such as:

> Be kind (Year 2)
>
> Sharing (Year 2)
>
> Being helpful (Year 3)
>
> A good person is someone who cares and is truthful and trustworthy (Year 4)
>
> A good person will help and care for everyone. A good person doesn't take sides. (Year 5)

When it came to the question 'How do you tell the difference between right and wrong?', however, there was a marked difference between the responses from children in Key Stage 1 and those in Key Stage 2:

> Bullying is wrong. Sharing is right (Year 2)
>
> If you do something right you get rewords and if you do a thing wrong you dont (Year 3)
>
> In assembly they tell us not to bully (Year 3)

> Right is when everybodys happy and all lives in peace Wrong is when people are being rude, lies, naughty, mean and harsh (Year 5)

> There isn't always a right and wrong and if there is you have to think carefully and decide. (Year 5)

The responses from the younger children do seem to tally with Piaget's notion that moral rules and expectations come from outside the child in the first instance, with adult instruction and use of reward systems playing their part here. The responses from the Year 5 children, however, seem to indicate some individual thought about what the aims of behaving well might be, about moral character, and, in the final response above, a realization that things are not always cut and dried when it comes to moral matters; strong indicators that these children might well be within the 'moral autonomy' stage of development. Interestingly, too, the responses (which came from both boys and girls) seem to indicate the development of both a morality of justice (in the references to sharing, truthfulness, trustworthiness and the importance of not taking sides) and a morality of care (in the references to helping, caring and being kind).

Children's development of empathy for others

The type of behaviour approved of in the responses by children cited above is often referred to as *pro-social behaviour*. Martin Hoffman (1970, 2000) suggested that the foundations for this are set as early as during the first year of life. During this time, Hoffman found, the expression of emotion (particularly crying and laughing) was a contagious behaviour; babies would cry when exposed to others' crying and laugh when exposed to others' laughter, a phenomenon that Hoffman terms 'global empathy' (Hoffman 1970: 42). According to Hoffman, this quite quickly led to babies' realization that children's crying had an association with unhappiness or distress, and children's laughter or pleasant gurgling (and so on) had an association with happiness and contentment. This is followed in the second year of life by an understanding that when another child cried, it was the *other* person who was upset, and a concern for alleviating this person's distress begins to show itself.

The key shift in children's understanding of other people's feelings is facilitated by the emergence and sharing of *language*; around the time most children are aged 3 they are using and responding to vocabulary and verbal expression that expresses particular emotions and feelings. Children from this age upwards are also typically engaged in lots of role-play and 'let's pretend' games (see Chapter 5 for more details). At its simplest, role-play can be understood as taking on the character or situation of someone else, or putting oneself in someone else's shoes, so it is not really surprising that children's ability to decentre and empathize is potentially developed strongly by this process – especially once ongoing language use is in the mix.

Children's understanding of other people and their feelings and perspectives on the world is also influenced strongly through the *stories* that surround them. If all is well – though, unfortunately, Ofsted's *Removing Barriers to Literacy* (2011) tells us it is often not – then children will be exposed to verbal story-telling, to books, to television programmes and DVDs, to stories that are family histories or predictions of future events, to stories that are other children's accounts of events that have occurred, and to the constant chitter-chatter of their parents or carers that is full of accounts of how people and things have made them feel. All of this exposure helps children develop empathy and understanding of others – in other words, they develop the ability to *decentre* that Piaget considered so important for moral development. More about stories will be said below.

Children's development of moral reasoning

The term *moral principles* refers to such things as respect for the sanctity of life, the importance of being truthful, the desire for fairness and fair treatment, the imperative to care for other people and treat them respectfully, and so on. *Moral reasoning* consists of the thinking and decision-making that children (and adults) go through to determine how, when, and to what extent the moral principles that they hold might be best applied. An example can be seen in a piece of conversation between two Year 4 boys involved in the research activities that included the question 'How do you tell the difference between right and wrong?', mentioned earlier:

> Boy A: At playtime Amy [name changed] came up to me and asked if I thought she was fat.
> Boy B: What did you say?
> Boy A: Well, actually, I *do* think she's a bit fat, but I said no so as not to upset her.

Two moral values seem to be in play here; the importance of telling the truth and the importance of looking after other people. What seems to have happened on this occasion is that Boy A prioritized the second of these moral principles over the first – in other words, he told a 'white lie', one that seemed to allow for the most desirable outcome to be reached.

Lawrence Kohlberg (1984) explored the development of such moral reasoning. He followed Piaget's approach to children's moral development in many ways and came up with a model of moral development that also suggested that it happened in stages and that the ability to appreciate other people's perspectives was crucial for sophisticated moral thinking. Kohlberg, like Piaget, considered that children started off as egocentric beings, unable to decentre and completely influenced by the moral values, norms and rules that emanated from the authority figures in their lives. Unlike Piaget, however, he determined that there were three distinct stages of morality, each of which could be broken down into two sub-stages, making six stages in all. For Kohlberg, which of these stages children were in depended very much on the way they reasoned about moral scenarios. Table 4.1 shows a simplified version of what Kohlberg's suggested stages look like.

Table 4.1   Kohlberg's (1984) six stages of moral development

Pre-conventional morality

Stage 1: Heteronomous morality	Children obey rules or expect to be punished.	Authorities determine what is good and bad. Children cannot decentre.
Stage 2: Instrumental morality	Children act out of self-interest when deciding to obey rules or norms of behaviour or not.	Children begin to appreciate fairness because it means they will not miss out compared to other people (as that would be unfair).

Conventional morality (from about age 7 or 8)

Stage 3: 'Good child' morality	Children can regulate their own behaviour without constant reinforcement from authority figures (though the norms and rules of behaviour still emanate from them).	Fairness becomes the *golden rule* – 'treat others as you would like to be treated yourself' (a simple version of Kant's categorical imperative). Children want to be seen and responded to as good. Children demonstrate caring attitudes and concern for others' well-being and happiness.
Stage 4: 'Law-and-order' morality	Children follow rules because the rules help the group operate smoothly.	Children find it important to maintain the social group.

Post-conventional morality (from about age 10 or 11)

Stage 5: 'Social contract' reasoning	Children moderate their behaviour to allow for the successful co-existence of people and groups with different opinions.	Children understand that different people can hold quite different moral principles and values, and approve of different behaviours.
Stage 6: Universal ethical principles	Children can justify and defend their own moral principles and explain how they might be applied to any situation.	Children can apply a variety of moral perspectives to any moral scenario and reason out desirable ways to proceed.

For Kohlberg, it was the type of moral reasoning (as explained above) that determined the stage children were in, more so than their actual behaviour. Kohlberg's key research technique was to give children stories that contained moral dilemmas and analyse the children's suggested solutions to these dilemmas and the reasons they offered for them. Piaget had previously used a similar technique to Kohlberg (though his stories were of comparative situations rather than dilemmas), and it was the reasoning that children offered for their responses that was of interest to Piaget too.

A consideration of some examples of Piaget's and Kohlberg's stories will demonstrate why this is so. One pair of stories offered by Piaget went as follows:

A. There was once a little girl who was called Marie. She wanted to give her mother a nice surprise, and cut out a piece of sewing for her. But she didn't know how to use the scissors properly and cut a big hole in her dress.

B. A little girl named Margaret went and took her mother's scissors one day that her mother was out. She played with them for a bit. Then as she didn't know how to use them properly she made a little hole in her dress.

(Piaget 1932/1965: 118)

Piaget asked children 'which of the two is naughtiest and why' (Piaget 1932/1965: 119). Children aged under 10 tended to say 'Marie', because the damage she had caused was more extensive; that is, they were more concerned with results than motives. Children aged over 10, however, had more sympathy for Marie, and tended to say that Margaret was the naughtier because Marie had been trying to do something nice for her mother; that is, they were more concerned with motives than results – something that, for Piaget, indicated a higher stage of moral reasoning and an ability to decentre.

Compare this to one of the stories Kohlberg used:

In Korea, a company of Marines was greatly outnumbered and was retreating before the enemy. The company had crossed a bridge over a river, but the enemy were still mostly on the other side. If someone went back to the bridge and blew it up as the enemy soldiers were coming over it, it would weaken the enemy. With the head start the rest of the men in the company would have, they could probably then escape. But the man who stayed back to blow up the bridge would probably not be able to escape alive; there would be about a 4 to 1 chance that he would be killed. The captain of the company has to decide who should go back and do the job. The captain is the man who knows best how to lead the retreat. He asks for volunteers, but no

one will volunteer. – Should the captain order a man to stay behind,
or stay behind himself, or leave nobody behind? Why?

(Kohlberg, cited in Duska and Whelan 1977: 122–123)

It can be seen that several possible moral principles might apply here: the imperative to preserve life, the need for fairness, the necessity to do one's duty, the requirement to use authority properly without abusing it, and the notion that the needs of the many outweigh the needs of the few (or the one, as *Star Trek* has it). It can also be seen that there are other purely cognitive issues to consider here, such as the judgement of which possible decision would give the group of men the best chance to survive. If one answers that the captain should leave nobody behind, then one is possibly somewhere in the 'conventional morality' stage, because this answer seems to be the simplest in terms of applying fairness to the whole group of men – never mind that their chances of survival are diminished as a consequence. If one answers that the captain himself should stay behind, then one is possibly entering the 'post-conventional morality' stage, because of the distaste of the notion that one should order another human being to meet his death, and that self-sacrifice is the better option. If one answers that the captain should order another soldier to go back, then one is either in the 'law-and-order' sub-stage of 'conventional morality' (because it is proper that authority exists and is exercised for the benefit of the group) or in the 'universal ethical principles' sub-stage of 'post-conventional morality' (because whoever goes back is likely to die anyway, whoever he is, so the most important thing is to give the rest of the group the best chance possible); this all depends on the sophistication of the reasons given for the answer.

Superheroes, stories, and children's moral development

All the moral dilemmas set by Kohlberg were of this nature; whichever option one chose out of those available would leave a bad taste in the mouth, and the trick was to choose the least worst option rather than attempt to satisfy every moral principle at once – something that each scenario made impossible. One of the great early appeals of superheroes, of course, is that their superpowers or other special abilities or gadgets would allow them to overcome many of the types of difficulty found in such scenarios; for example, in the Korea story above Superman could destroy the bridge from a distance with his heat vision, or Invisible Woman could create an invisible force field to prevent the enemy getting through, or Storm from the X-Men could literally raise a storm to hinder the enemy, or Green Lantern could create a huge green hand to carry the troops out of danger, and so on. In other words, the existence of superheroes would allow for the greatest good to be achieved for all without anyone having to suffer or any moral principle needing to be compromised. One reason that children engage with superheroes through play and story is that they offer a sort of moral wish-fulfilment: superheroes can make everything all right for everybody (at least in terms of physical danger), and many young children are naturally good-hearted and want the world to be fine and life to be happy for everyone.

As they develop, children can engage with more complex superhero stories that do involve moral dilemmas and require more advanced moral reasoning: here are two examples. In the seminal film *Superman* (1978), Superman has to choose which of two missiles he stops, knowing that he cannot stop both at the same time. Similarly, he has a choice of whether he rescues Lois (whom he loves) first, or not. Superman elects to first save a train from derailing, a school bus from falling off a bridge, and a town from being flooded, with the result that when he returns to Lois it seems that he is too late to save her. Did he make the (morally) right choice? Children could also meet the character 'Two-Face', who appears in many Batman stories. Two-Face flips a coin to choose between possible courses of action, which are often presented as choices between good and evil. Children's moral reasoning will be exercised as they consider what they think of this character's abdication of moral responsibility and his seeming contentment to follow courses of action that he knows are evil if the coin dictates that he should.

Superheroes and their stories are all posited around morality; Chapter 8 will show in more detail how they are full of the exploration of moral values and principles, of caring for others, of ideas about the 'greater good', of what it is to be a good character and act well. Superheroes themselves are constituted around their moral positions rather than their powers (as, indeed, are supervillains), and have much capacity to act as strong role models and authority figures for children in how they approach the world morally (for example, as well as officially being 'the man of steel', Superman is also 'the last boy scout' – a reference to his moral steadfastness and character). For these reasons, as most of the rest of the book will demonstrate, children's engagement with superheroes and superhero play has the potential to be of great service to their ongoing development of moral principles, values and reasoning.

5 From 'rough-and-tumble' play to superhero and conflict play

Introduction

One of the possible problems with the existing category of 'war, weapon and superhero play' is that this category puts together many different types of play that children can engage in as if they were aspects of one and the same thing. Levin and Carlsson-Paige (2006), for example, consistently refer to 'war and superhero play' as a single entity, while Holland (2003) uses the term 'war, weapon and superhero play' as an overarching category to include all the examples of play that she discusses. It is at least possible that the many different types of play potentially engaged in under the heading 'war, weapon and superhero play' might benefit from being looked at separately, as each is likely to have its own characteristics, and putting them together as if they were automatically part of the same phenomenon might lead some aspects of them being missed; for example, superhero play can take the form of a very physical 'rough-and-tumble' type of play, imaginative role-play scenarios involving themes such as rescue or good versus evil, the exploration of fantasy powers (such as invisibility or flight), or playing *Superhero Squad* or *Batman: The Brave and the Bold* games (and so on) on a Nintendo DS machine. It is also worth observing here that these types of play might include aspects of weaponry (such as pretend batarangs – the bat-shaped throwing weapon used by Batman – or rockets fired from a superhero vehicle and so forth) but equally they might very well not: a child moving around a reception class under an imagined cloak of invisibility might be engaging in a form of superhero play, but not a form of weapons play; similarly, a group of children moving around or chasing each other with Lego guns would clearly be playing a form of weapon play, but such play need not involve any reference to superhero characters or scenarios whatsoever.

If there were to be an overarching term to describe this range of play, then I would suggest that *superhero and conflict play* might improve upon 'war, weapon and superhero play'. Much superhero play involves imagined conflict between good and evil (see Chapter 8) whether it utilizes pretend weapons or not, and the removal of an implied automatic link between superhero play and weapon play might be of service in pursuing understanding of both types of play.

Where superhero and conflict play might start: rough-and-tumble play

Much superhero play involves a very large element of physicality – for example, chasing, running, leaping, grappling and play-fighting, things which are commonly categorized as elements of *rough-and-tumble play*. Many reasons for the existence of such play have been offered, and it would be useful to explore several of these in some detail.

A common observation of rough-and-tumble play is that it seems much more common among boys than girls (see Cohen 2006; Jarvis 2009). This leads to the first type of explanation offered for such play: that it is a form of practice for activity in later life, and the roles and range of behaviours that we seem to be evolutionarily programmed for. This idea was first put forward by Groos (1901), who drew attention to the way that, for example, lion and tiger cubs could often be seen chasing, pushing and pretend-fighting with each other – behaviour that acted as a precursor to the hunting, defending and attempting to establish dominance over others that they would carry out when fully grown members of their species. More recently, authors such as Bjorklund and Pellegrini (2002) and Ridley (2004) have suggested that we are born with a kind of in-built evolutionary model of behaviour; that our behaviour can be understood to a great extent as a manifestation of our evolutionary drives. These evolutionary drives give patterns to our behaviour, including the types of practice play we exhibit during our childhoods; we practise our own food-collecting, defending of territory and tribe or family, and nurturing of those younger than ourselves.

Many commentators argue that these evolutionary imperatives are gendered in nature, so the main reason that boys seem more drawn to rough-and-tumble play than girls is, according to authors such as Sax (2009) and Gurian and Stevens (2007), because they have inherited quite different evolutionary drives to girls. As Palmer (2009: 6) puts it:

> The sorts of masculine behaviour required for stalking, pursuing and killing wild animals are very different from the feminine virtues needed for raising infants and getting along with one's fellow campers. Natural selection therefore meant that over the millennia, male and female developed gender traits fitting them for their particular roles, and these traits are hard-wired into our psyches from birth.

From this perspective, then, rough-and-tumble play can be understood as a manifestation of children's natural selves and instinctive behaviours, and the predominant appeal of this type of play to boys also seems to be explained to some extent. Children engaged in this form of play are, it seems, giving expression to some of the deepest evolutionary drives that inform their nature as members of the human species. Common aspects of superhero and conflict play such as running, chasing, play-fighting and play-defending, therefore, can be partially accounted for by this idea.

It is worth pointing out, however, that rough-and-tumble play remains *play*; in other words, that the mixture of play-chasing, play-fighting and play-defending often involved is a form of let's-pretend rather than an expression of genuine aggression. Rough-and-tumble play seems to be co-operative and mutually satisfying in nature (see Jarvis 2009) and often quite affectionate. For example, one father described the rough-and-tumble play that frequently took place between him and his 5-year-old son:

> We roll around the carpet and pretend to doof each other. Sometimes one of us will say something like 'Now I've got you!' in an exaggerated voice, and the other one will say 'No you haven't!' or something like that. [. . .] will often ask me to have a 'fight' with him, but we never actually hurt each other, of course – except sometimes he gets me by accident. In actual fact, we both take great pains to make sure that neither of us gets hurt for real. Sometimes he asks his mummy to join in, but she doesn't really, or, at least, only to join in a throwing-bean-bags-at-each-other-gently type of game. It's a Daddy-and-[. . .] thing, really.

This is not to say that rough-and-tumble play can never escalate into something that seems to have more of an aggressive character to it than is desirable, but this seems to be when children have been carried away with the excitement of the game, or when the ground rules that are in place for any kind of play are not communicated or enforced sufficiently clearly or consistently. Aggression and rough-and-tumble play remain two different phenomena (Pellegrini 2006). More will be said about how to prevent such an escalation at the end of this chapter.

The valuable physicality of superhero and conflict play

It also seems likely that there are more immediate drives underpinning rough-and-tumble play and other forms of superhero and conflict play. Any inherited deep-seated evolutionary drives such as those identified above are complemented by the ongoing daily need that children have to exercise their bodies and develop them physically. Much activity and play in the early years consists of actions that practise and apply both gross motor skills (such as crawling, jumping, running and climbing) and fine motor skills (for example, manipulating tools such as paintbrushes, doing up buttons, threading and – eventually – writing). Children in the early years seem to be constantly engaged in physical movement if given their own way (which is not always the case as children pass through Reception and into Year 1). Movement and physical exercise are necessary for children to remain healthy and develop healthily – which is why physical development is now a Prime Area of Learning and Development in the EYFS. The previous version of the EYFS also acknowledged the importance of physical development:

> The physical development of . . . young children must be encouraged through the provision of opportunities for them to be active and interactive and to improve their skills of coordination, control, manipulation and movement. They must be supported in using all of their senses to learn about the world around them.
>
> (DCSF 2008b: 92)

Superhero and conflict play gives children the opportunity to pretend to be characters who express themselves largely through physical movement: Superman, Tommy Zoom, Storm and many, many others fly; Spider-Man climbs up walls and swings on webs; Batman swoops down with his cape swishing around him; Iceman slides on icy pathways generated from his body; Hulk and She-Hulk smash their way through walls; the Flash moves at superspeed; Thor swings his hammer; *Star Wars* characters joust with light-sabres. Virtually all superheroes and superhero and conflict play narratives involve huge amounts of larger-than-life physical action, which is a deep and integral part of their appeal. Consider this extract from an interview conducted with a West Sussex nursery manager, for example:

Me: What do you think the appeal was [of superhero play]?
Nursery Manager: I think it was the opportunity to run around, and knowing that the things he watched on television and films and stuff that they [superheroes] were very fast-acting. Obviously they flew, a lot of them, and it was just something that he wasn't able to do, but it was something that he depicted quite often; charging around the garden with one arm out in front of the other. We have a large trampoline, and very often you'd find him jumping up in the air, you know, 'I'm Superman, I'm flying', kind of scenario . . . He would fly everywhere and rescue everybody.

More will be said about the 'rescuing everybody' scenario and its moral dimensions in Chapter 8, but what this illustrates for now is that children involved in superhero and conflict play have engaged themselves in a context that actively encourages and delights in large-scale and dynamic physical activity. Superhero play provides a very capable vehicle for children's imaginative and often joyous physical expression.

The importance of physical movement is not restricted to ensuring the body's healthy development. Piaget and Inhelder (1969: 4) identified that young children have a 'sensori-motor intelligence' that almost completely shapes their cognitive development until the emergence of language around the age of 2. Children learn through their physical and sensory explorations of the environment that surrounds them, the objects in this environment and the motor activities brought to bear on these objects and environment. As children repeat types of action and experience the physical consequences and sensations of these actions they begin to notice patterns in their experiences: action X always causes consequence or sensation Y. This can be illustrated through consideration of a marble-run game; a marble dropped down one particular tube will behave the same way as a marble dropped down that same tube two seconds earlier or one second later. The marble will always seek to travel downwards, and will do so until its passage is blocked. Similarly, a teddy-bear will always feel softer to hold than a wooden brick. It is through constant movement and physical engagement with the world that children begin to learn about the properties of the world that they engage with, and about their own physical characteristics, abilities and sensations too. The capability to detect patterns and consistencies in the way the physical world behaves eventually leads to developments in children's abilities to categorize, compare, predict, and so on – the building blocks of what Piaget and Inhelder (1969) considered to be the ability to *think*.

It is also worth acknowledging that physical play and behaviour seem to be different between boys and girls (at least typically – it is important to recognize that any generalized assertions here might not automatically apply to individual children). According to authors such as Sax (2009) and Gurian and Stevens (2007), boys and girls have different innate sets of biological and physiological needs, characteristics and behaviours, and their physical play is one avenue where these can find expression. Commentators such as Sax (2005), James (2007) and Gurian and Stevens (2007) observe that parts of boys' brains develop in different ways and at different speeds than girls' brains, and seem to be utilized differently by girls and boys as they mature; phenomena that are offered as reasons for the differences boys and girls typically demonstrate in, for example, verbal and spatial abilities (Baron-Cohen 2004). Boys and girls have a different mix of hormones coursing through their systems, particularly testosterone and oestrogen, and are subject to their different effects (Maccoby and Jacklin 1974). Boys and girls are built differently physically, as can be seen in their different musculature and secondary sexual characteristics, which, according to Kail (2010: 414), means that 'boys tend to be bigger, stronger, and more active; girls tend to have better fine-motor coordination and to be healthier'. Put together, these things might also be reasons why superhero and conflict play commonly seems to appeal more strongly to boys than to girls, as such play often involves a kind of large-scale accented physicality that might resonate more closely with boys who are more in tune with gross-motor activity than with girls more interested in fine-motor pursuits.

How superhero and conflict play develops: imaginative and symbolic play

The possible limitation of the explanations for superhero and conflict play given above, however, is that they might reduce such play to something that does not necessarily have to involve individual thought or choice, but is just a manifestation of unconscious evolutionary or physical drives. Children, however, are conscious and individual thinking beings, and in order to understand their play one has to take into account children's own unique choices and interests too. Piaget (1962) helps us again here with a different way of understanding play-as-practice (the notion that this discussion began with). For Piaget, early play (from birth until the emergence of language around the age of 2) is dominated by a mixture of a re-creation of familiar processes and events and an emulation of behaviour witnessed; in other words, children start off by practising things which are much more immediate than inherited evolutionary behaviour patterns. Children will witness literal activities such as cooking, driving, running, posting letters, hugging, getting dressed, and so on, and versions of such things might find representation in their play. They will witness the various degrees of affection or disapproval that seem embedded in the behaviour of people who surround them. They will also witness the roles that different people seem to adopt and the behaviours that correspond to these roles. Early years dressing-up and role-play games can often reflect such things – a child playing out the role of a mother might comfort or pretend to feed her teddies, dolls or play companions, or, indeed, might tell them off in a way representative of that experienced in real life.

As children pass between 2 and 6 years old, they inhabit what Piaget (1962) considered the second of three stages of play. This stage sees children deeply involved in make-believe and symbolic play; play is no longer limited to literal re-creation but becomes open-ended and fantastical. The imaginative scenarios that might inform any play experience can vastly extend beyond the here-and-now; children can explore different worlds, battle against dragons, use magic, turn into other characters and so on. A child might pick up a pen and, in his or her head, transform that pen into an aeroplane, a magic wand, a light-sabre, a gun, a device that turns him or her invisible, a batarang, a healing stick, a lever that opens the door to the dungeon. It is the *meaning* that the child attaches to the object being played with and how it is used that is now of importance – as also pointed out by Vygotsky (1978).

Significantly, though, children in this stage are still involved in forms of practice-play, except that what they are practising now is *possibility*. In addition, all the fantastical scenarios and narratives that might get created and explored will still involve children practising role and relationship; for example, if a girl takes on the role of a mother during such play, then her make-believe play version of what it is to be a mother will still represent her knowledge and understanding of *real-life* mothering in a logical and coherent fashion. The difference is that her pretending-to-be-a-mother play is not limited to re-enactments of actual occurrences but is now completely open-ended; the girl can cognitively and emotionally explore how a mother might be and might act in a whole range of real-life and fantastical scenarios. Not only that, but she will select and explore the aspects of a mother's nature and behaviour and the types of scenario that are *significant to her*.

Consider this example of superhero play carried out by a 4-year-old girl in a West Sussex Reception class earlier this year. Children in the class were engaged in a sequence of activities that invited them to create, share ideas about, and draw superheroes that they might like to be, and then utilize these creations in a piece of whole-class drama led by the teacher. This particular girl created a superhero whom she called 'Super Mum', whose power was to fly and whose mission was to 'make people better'. The girl utilized the superhero activities in a way that let her explore and express ideas about what seemed to be a key aspect of real-life mothering to her; the girl, in the guise of 'Super Mum', could now fly to people who needed help and look after them even more quickly and immediately. The pretend flying and superhero conceit remained fantastical, but the administering of care replicated that experienced in real life, with the added benefit that hardly any response time was needed at all before 'Super Mum' arrived to make people better – something that might have represented the desire for or appreciation of her own mother's perceived ability to be on hand whenever the need arose.

Once children reach this stage of play, then, superhero and conflict play can be utilized by children to explore ideas, possibilities, themes and scenarios that are of personal, individual and *conscious* significance or interest to them. These themes and scenarios might concern ideas about personal identity (see Chapter 7), or moral issues and character (see Chapter 8), or shared cultural experiences, expectations and stories (see Chapters 6 and 11). Similarly, these themes and scenarios could range from the very basic to ones of remarkable sophistication. Superhero and conflict play cannot be completely accounted for by explanations that concentrate on evolutionary drives or physiological and biological characteristics and needs. There is potentially something more individual, conscious and complex at work too.

Superhero and conflict play invites children to engage with a hugely varied cast of dynamic, well-defined and larger-than-life characters, to delight in and express themselves through accentuated physical action, and to explore scenarios that frequently concern the restoration of the good, the protection of the innocent, or the struggle between heroes and villains (as children understand such characters to be – see Chapter 8). As such it offers huge potential for children's sophisticated immersion in what has been termed *socio-dramatic play*; in other words, play that involves the adoption of character, the use of dramatically appropriate language to bring different characters to life, and a mutual and co-operative development of an underpinning, internally consistent storyline through the combination of verbal communication and physical movement. Socio-dramatic play has long been recognized for its vast potential to support and promote children's cognitive development because of the exercise of these combined elements (see Smilansky 1990). Moreover, socio-dramatic play involves children in expressing their own views and responding to their playmates' views about the way their play evolves, as well as perspectives of the characters they and their playmates pretend to be. In other words, socio-dramatic play strongly supports and informs children's developing ability to *decentre*, something that seems crucial for children's moral understanding and sensitivities to develop (as explained in the previous chapter).

Such play also has the potential to support and promote children's emotional development too. The 'Super Mum' illustration above demonstrates how children's emotional attachments to significant figures in their lives can find expression in socio-dramatic superhero play, for example. More generally, Singer (1994: 12) concluded that children 'who played more often at make-believe . . . [were] more likely to smile and laugh . . . [be] more persistent, more cooperative, and less likely to be angry, aggressive, or sad'. Altogether, then, it seems that superhero and conflict play might offer teachers and early years professionals a very productive resource indeed.

Behaviour management of superhero and conflict play

As discussed in Chapter 1, many teachers and other early years professionals are understandably anxious about any form of weapon play or play that engages children in play scenarios that involve them in pretend violence of any sort. Responses include blanket banning approaches (see Holland 2003), strategies that attempt to shape such play in directions regarded as more fruitful and positive by the professionals in charge (see Levin and Carlsson-Paige 2006), and a more permissive approach that allows children to shape and direct their play as they see fit.

When some form of weapon or pretend-violence play is present, then it becomes important to set clear ground rules for it that allow the children to continue and develop their play in ways that seem important to them, and that ensure the safety and security of the children participating in such play, as well as those not participating in the play, but exposed to it and within range of it.

It is suggested that the key ground rule to set is that no one must be hurt for real as a result of the play, and that any such outcome will result in the termination of the game for individual children or even the whole group when appropriate. Professionals can be firm about this expectation and their response to it, but what is important is that *harm to children* is discouraged rather than the whole form of play itself. If children find it difficult to play without harming other children accidentally, then it might be beneficial to outlaw certain aspects of the play (for example, if children seem to play-aim blows to other children's heads, then this particular feature of the game could be banned rather than the entirety of the play). Enforcing this central ground rule in this manner is also useful because it gives children the possibility of maintaining and developing their play, but in a more socially acceptable manner, and, importantly, the moral responsibility to adjust and control their behaviour for themselves, rather than having all discretion taken away from them (which, of course, would be the result of blanket banning rather than selective banning). Obviously, though, if any child hurts or upsets someone else deliberately, then that should be the immediate end of that particular child's playing of the game.

The second key ground rule suggested is that children should check that other children wish to join in the game before involving them in it or aiming the game their way. For example, one nursery worker pointed to an example of a group of children who would aim the firearms they pretended to have at other children elsewhere in the room and say 'bang!', which the children aimed at could find distressing or unpleasant. The nursery adopted this ground rule, with the result that the children took more control over whom they aimed any pretend guns or physical actions towards, and acted with increased sensitivity towards the group as a whole.

The third key ground rule concerns language use. Children involved in socio-dramatic superhero and conflict play might well use vocabulary or a tone of voice that possibly reflects the characters they are pretending to be or the oppositional scenario that these characters might be engaged in. Even so, they need to ensure that the language they use is still appropriate for the nursery or classroom setting. Any terms that the professionals involved judge as likely to be too crude, violent or potentially worrying to other children (whether within or outside the game) probably *are*, so professionals need to ensure that this ground rule is followed through. Children are likely to benefit from having any particular terms of vocabulary or phrases banned (or receiving advice about using an appropriate tone of voice) if any real issue in this area has arisen in practice.

The next ground rule suggested is really a variant on 'children should look where they are going'. In other words, since large-scale physical movement is commonly a feature of superhero and conflict play, children should take care not to crash into other children or the resources that they are using, or interfere with other children's use of space.

The final rule to suggest is not really a rule of behaviour but a rule of thumb. As discussed earlier, rough-and-tumble play is often collaborative and affectionate in nature and, like all forms of play, feels like it is *fun*. If the play witnessed seems to lack sufficient mutuality or feel imposed on any children, then it is probably time to remind the children of the ground rules suggested here. Certainly, if the play feels like it has crossed the line into something featuring genuine aggression, then it should be stopped – or, at least, those participants who seem to exhibit signs of aggression should be removed from it. Communicating clear and consistent expectations about this will mean that the children soon learn what the acceptable boundaries of superhero and conflict play are, for the benefit of the entire group.

It will be observed that all these ground rules are rather defensive – in other words, that they deal with productive professional responses to situations that are at risk of going wrong. The most productive approach, of course, is to utilize such rules within a rich narrative and activity-based context which has already been developed to facilitate thoughtful types of superhero and conflict play that can actively promote mutuality, co-operation and the development of empathy. The next chapter will discuss how all these valuable things can be promoted through the vehicle of children's superhero and conflict play.

6 Superhero and conflict play and the development of co-operation, empathy and sense of community

Introduction

A group of Year 5 and Year 6 children have been intrigued by a game brought in by the teacher to be used as part of some work developing children's thinking skills. *Death Angel*, as the game is called, is essentially a card game, but also involves throwing a specially designed dice (Konieczka 2010). It can be played by up to six players, and on this occasion four children have elected to try it out (with the teacher taking care of some of the mechanics of the game, but not interfering with the children's choices of which cards they will play or how they will play them). The game is based in Games Workshop's popular *Warhammer 40,000* universe, and revolves around the scenario of (in this case) eight 'space marines' – fantastical futuristic soldiers – attempting to board a spaceship that is derelict save for the presence of deadly alien monsters. Each player is responsible for one team of these super-soldiers, while the monsters and their activities are generated by cards that get revealed.

If any of the space marines survive through five spaceship locations then the threat posed by the monsters is eliminated and the space marines (in other words, the players) win. If, on the other hand, the space marines fail to make it that far, then the monsters win, mankind remains in peril, and all the players lose. Near the beginning of the game, while all eight of the space marines are intact, they have some chance of success; however, the odds against them rise geometrically with each loss of a man on the way. The game can easily reach a tipping-point which sees the few remaining space marines surrounded, outnumbered and utterly helpless to defend themselves against certain death.

As is probably already clear by now, the imagery, language and narrative of the game are entirely violent. Individual space marines are described or evoked on their cards with statements such as 'Only one thing matters to Brother Leon in battle – kill count' and 'Brother Kaphael assaults the enemy with discipline and wisdom'. The key activity being imagined is 'kill or be killed', with the space marines and monsters taking turns to attack. Getting through to the final location typically requires all the monsters to be killed, or the source of their existence being blown up, or the most powerful monsters to be destroyed, and so on.

The children start the game optimistically, and the teacher keeps an eye on the strategies that they use. He notices that the children start off by only reinforcing space marines in their own teams rather than the ones whose positioning means that they are most at threat and most in need of such reinforcement. He also notices some bickering when children move their own teams of men in a way that leaves the other children's teams of men disadvantaged and exposed. The bickering is not so much because any children's space marines have ended up in a worse situation; rather, it is because some children's soldiers have been moved without consultation, explanation or permission. Similarly, when the children get their space marines to attack any monsters early in the game their attack tends to be aimed at any monsters threatening their own team rather than the ones posing the most threat to the space marines overall.

It is not long before the various teams of space marines begin to be decimated, with the few that are left quickly overwhelmed and defeated. The game breaks up in acrimony. The teacher allows a few moments for the children to let off steam, then sits with them and calms them down. He shares his observations of the way the children approached the game and the way they played their cards and offers a few pointers. He suggests that they could try again after playtime once they have thought a bit and shared their reflections on the game and how they played it.

Once the children have calmed down and returned, the group take up the teacher's offer and begin the game again. This time a different approach is evident. First of all, they talk to each other about how they are thinking of playing the cards, and they listen to each other. Secondly, they play the cards quite differently. The soldiers who need reinforcement are reinforced, regardless of which child's team they are part of. The space marines are moved with much more consideration of their overall deployment, regardless of how the individual teams end up being placed. The children concentrate their forces on protecting the most powerful space marines and attacking the swarms of monsters that present the greatest threat.

This time they win the game, and there are smiles all around. They share pleasantries about how much fun the game was and offer each other compliments about the way they played particular cards at particular times. They enjoy telling the other children in the class that they won, and represent themselves as a *team* while doing so. The collaborative and co-operative nature of their second attempt at the game has paid dividends.

This example illustrates the way that co-operation can be nurtured even in play that is based around a very violent, oppositional or weapons-heavy premise. The narrative that gave flavour to the card game was full of battle and death-dealing, yet the actual play ended up being collaborative and mutually respectful.

The rest of this chapter will explore this potential further. It will look at how the actual narratives that can lie behind superhero and conflict play are often full of themes about the value of co-operation, empathy and teamwork, before turning its attention to more examples of how teachers and early years professionals have promoted and developed children's co-operation and empathy through utilizing superhero and conflict play in particular ways.

How superheroes explore and promote co-operation, teamwork, camaraderie and empathy for others

Superheroes rarely exist alone. Most superheroes are situated in a context that includes family, loved ones, friends, work colleagues, and, of course, other superheroic or even normal human allies. Many superheroes operate in teams, such as the Fantastic Four, the Justice League, the X-Men and the Avengers. For the younger children (say, between ages 3 and 8) two particular incarnations of superheroes represented in current DVDs, electronic games and supermarket comics place teamwork and co-operation at their centre. DC's *Batman: The Brave and the Bold* (a modern young-child-friendly revamp of a comic from the 1960s and 1970s) features Batman teaming up on a rotational basis with various other superheroes such as Aquaman, Green Lantern, Plastic Man and Power Girl. Marvel's *Superhero Squad* features a host of superheroes such as Thor, the Hulk, the Falcon, Invisible Woman, Firestar and Wolverine, all of whom are based in 'Superhero City' and led equally by Ms. Marvel and Iron Man (who gets to say 'Hero up!' to the rest of the 'squaddies').

Virtually all of the stories that involve such teams of superheroes centre around the social, emotional and, especially, moral dynamics of the particular groups. Typically, the stories told about these groups cast the various characters into certain social, moral and emotional roles, and it is the interaction of characters in these roles that determines how the groups operate as teams. The actual composition of most superhero groups varies over time, but some examples of the typical roles that characters take on are shown in Table 6.1.

It is worth noting that none of these roles would be available in quite the same way when superheroes are acting alone; for example, it is only when there is a group of characters working together that someone can take on a leadership role, or be dependent on the support or direction of others. Dramatizing characters' interactions with each other allows stories involving teams of superheroes to explore, in lively and vibrant ways, themes of loyalty, responsibility, common purpose, moral decision-making and looking after one another. The various moral or emotional standpoints explored during any story are brought to life through the characters' dialogue and their behaviour towards each other.

Table 6.1 Group roles in superhero team stories

Role in group	Superhero character	Group
The calm, rational one (commonly the leader of the group)	Mr. Fantastic	Fantastic Four
	Professor X	X-Men
	The Martian Manhunter/Superman (at different times)	Justice League
The caring one	The Invisible Woman	Fantastic Four
	Phoenix (Jean Grey)	X-Men
	Wonder Woman	Justice League
The angry one (typically the maverick of the group)	The Thing	Fantastic Four
	Wolverine	X-Men
	Green Lantern (Guy Gardner version)	Justice League
The determined one	Mr. Fantastic	Fantastic Four
	Cyclops	X-Men
	Batman	Justice League
The young, impetuous one	The Human Torch	Fantastic Four
	Iceman	X-Men
	Hawkgirl	Justice League
The vulnerable one	Franklin (Reed and Sue Richard's young son)	Fantastic Four
	Jubilee and Kitty Pryde	X-Men
	Hawkgirl	Justice League

As with all good drama, the different characters act as foils for each other, with some individuals' natural instincts or behaviour being tempered by the responses of the other individuals around them. An example of a typical interaction between a leader figure (Mr. Fantastic in this case) and an angry figure (the Thing) demonstrates this very well. In this particular story Ben Grimm (the Thing) has acted very aggressively towards the Silver Surfer because of an unnecessary jealousy over what he misunderstands as the Silver Surfer's attempts to seduce his girlfriend. The child reader knows that no such attempts have been made at all, and that the threat to the relationship is all in Ben Grimm's head. Finally, Mr. Fantastic has had enough:

> Mr. Fantastic: Get that *chip* off your shoulder, big fella, before I *knock* it off . . . and you've got me itching to *do* it, too! I thought you were in love with Alicia . . . but instead, you've left her crying her eyes out!
>
> The Thing: Sure! Over that crummy *Silver Surfer*!
>
> Invisible Woman: Oh, *no*, Ben . . . *No*!
>
> Mr. Fantastic: When are you gonna *grow up*, Grimm? Or are you trying to prove you're really as dumb as you *look*? The *Surfer* doesn't mean

anything to Alicia . . . he's not even *human*! She felt *sorry* for him . . . that's all! It's *you* she's worried about! She was afraid you'd be *injured* . . . fighting over *nothing*!

The Thing: I wouldn't let *no one* talk to me like you just did, Mister . . . 'Less mebbe I knew . . . deep down . . . that yer *right*!

Mr. Fantastic: Now *listen*, Ben . . . we've been friends for years . . . I'd give my *life* for you . . . and you *know* it! But, you big, blister-brained baboon, if you don't *apologize* to him for acting like a misanthropic *madman*, I'll show you what clobbering really *means*!!

The Thing: Awright . . . awright! I git the message! I acted like a *chump*!

(Lee and Kirby 1966: 66)

The dialogue leads the child reading the story through the important moral and emotional aspects of the story step-by-step in a very accessible manner: there has been no just cause for the Thing's violence so it needs to stop and be apologized for; Alicia has been concerned for the well-being of her boyfriend, and this has made her upset and tearful, a situation that needs remedying; the Thing accepts moral responsibility for his own actions; and, most significantly, Mr. Fantastic clearly expresses his strong opinion that Ben's behaviour that has been at fault (and that Ben needs to make amends for it), but also that he (Mr. Fantastic) still loves Ben and is loyal to him as deeply as he ever was. (An equivalent process can be seen in many classrooms, where teachers and early years professionals take pains to reject what they see as any child's poor behaviour, but do so in a way that does not also reject the child.)

It is also significant that Mr. Fantastic, who is usually calm and rational in all situations, gets angry and emotional with Ben. This in itself demonstrates to the child how important resolving the situation is, both emotionally and morally – just as teachers and early years professionals raise their voices or use stern language only when they judge it to be absolutely necessary because of the severity of any behavioural situation.

This is only one example of the way that superhero team stories can explore moral scenarios and emotional situations. There are plenty of stories that involve the young impetuous member of the group dashing off and causing poor and unforeseen consequences by acting before thinking (an important moral message for children) and requiring the superhero group to somehow put the pieces back together again. There are stories that involve the vulnerable member(s) of the group either being threatened or receiving an emotional knock-back, which requires the rest of the group to offer protection or emotional support. There are stories where the leader of the group explains the moral principles or issues that are at stake, ostensibly for the benefit of the rest of the group, but really for the benefit of the reader or viewer. There are stories where the maverick, angry member of the group is prevented from doing something rash or ill-judged by the more even-tempered others in the group – and, conversely, stories where the weight of feeling (often moral outrage) expressed by the maverick figure galvanizes the rest of the team into action. There are stories where the most caring figure of the group – often female, which is interesting given Gilligan's (1982) notion that it is women who most develop and exhibit a morality of care – nurtures and looks after another character's feelings and physical well-being. There are stories where the firm determination expressed by one character overcomes the sense of helplessness or failure experienced by other members of the team. There are stories where the heroes only overcome the overwhelming danger by pulling together as a team (while, typically, opposing teams of villains fall apart in rancour and disagreement as things increasingly go wrong for them). There are many, many stories that involve one member of the team being trapped and at high risk and the others refusing to leave him or her behind despite the likelihood that no one will get out unscathed, or even at all.

Tellingly, there are a substantial number of superhero stories where the harm intended by the villain is the disharmony and break-up of the superhero group itself; for example, the 2007 *Fantastic Four* film (Frost and France 2007) centres around a plot-line which sees Doctor Doom's sly and extended attempt to deceive and misrepresent individual members of the Fantastic Four so that they lose trust in one another and turn upon themselves. (Needless to say, it is the four members of the Fantastic Four's eventual teamwork and reaffirmation of themselves as a loyal and united group that overcomes Doctor Doom in the end.) This type of story is really shorthand for an exploration of the desire that some people have for the purposeful break-up and destruction of the community in which they live or other communities that they fear or hate or are jealous of – certainly a theme for our times. The desired good expressed by such stories is the re-establishment of the community's wholeness, ability to work together harmoniously, and belief in its individual members – things which make up the core of the Citizenship curriculum in school (and the more traditional subject of Ethics too).

Children who engage with superheroes and their narratives soak up such stories and all their emotional and moral content almost automatically. Bruner (1986: 16) points out that all 'narrative deals with the vicissitudes of human intentions', and stories like these, while fantastical in terms of superpowers, costumes and plot-lines (and so on) are still posited around real-life human motivations, emotions and moral decision-making. This is a similar realization to that of MacIntyre (1981: 216), who concluded that: 'It is through hearing stories . . . that children learn or mislearn . . . what the cast of characters may be in the drama into which they have been born and what the ways of the world are.' In other words, children who engage with superheroes and their narratives might be immersed in a fantasy world, but at the heart of this world lie potential insights into what makes people tick and what spurs them on to be good (or otherwise) to each other.

It is very rare for any superhero story to not have such a moral or emotional centre. Even superhero stories for the youngest children contain such things; for example, a recent issue of *Spider-Man and Friends* (2011) – which is aimed at children in the Foundation Stage – involves a story set in a school which all the superpowered characters attend (in this comic they are portrayed as 5- or 6-year-old versions of the normal depictions). The plot-line of this story involves Doctor Octopus playing a series of practical jokes on the rest of the characters, such as placing a giant pretend spider on Wolverine's desk and putting a comic hairband on top of Captain America's cowl without him realizing (the gentle level of wrongdoing offered to pre-school children). The story ends with Spider-Man working out who is behind the pranks: 'So Doc decides to stop playing pranks and play with his friends instead. "Can I join in your race?" he asks. "Of course you can", Spidey agrees' (Hoskin 2011: 5). Once again – and for the youngest of children this time – it is the reaffirmation and reintegration of the whole group and the inclusion of all its members (even the rather naughty Doctor Octopus) that is the key moral theme at hand.

Very importantly, however, there are also stories that involve good superhero characters making difficult but well-intended moral choices, the consequences of which turn out to be bad for the superhero team and its individual members. These stories explore the moral dimensions and consequences of these difficult moral choices and, potentially, shed even more light on the effects that one character's actions can have on others, for good or ill. One particular example comes to mind.

The animated X-Men story *Till Death Do Us Part* (Edens 1993/2009, broadcast as part of a Saturday morning children's television show on ITV in March 2012) sees the X-Men deceived and beaten by a shape-changing character that we eventually discover is really Morph. Morph is a former member of the X-Men, long thought dead. During a previous adventure (which we see part of in flashback) he was trapped and apparently killed while the rest of the X-Men had to make a strategic retreat – the difficult but well-intended choice of action. What we now discover is that Morph's unconscious body was taken by the aptly named Mr. Sinister, who then brainwashed Morph and somehow corrupted his identity while he recovered. The damaged Morph now believes (with some justification) that he was abandoned and left to die by the X-Men and has been ordered by Mr. Sinister to destroy them; however, the part of him that remains truly himself struggles with this:

Morph: No! They were all my friends! I don't want to hurt them. Arghh!
         But why did they abandon me? Why did they leave me to die?
Mr. Sinister's voice: You will destroy them all.
Morph: I will destroy them all!

(Edens 1993/2009)

Once Morph has helped Mr. Sinister defeat the X-Men he is confronted by Wolverine and the others:

> Wolverine: I know you feel betrayed, Morph. After we were whipped by the Sentinels I tried to make Cyclops go back for you. Cyclops had to leave you behind to save the rest of us. Maybe he was wrong, but that's no reason for revenge.
>
> Morph: Who are you trying to convince? Me or yourself?
>
> Jean Grey: Cyclops did what he had to do for the good of the team – what you would have done in his place.
>
> Morph: That's easy for you to say!
>
> Cyclops: Morph – you gotta help us! Whatever happens, you're still part of the team – still one of the X-Men!
>
> Morph: One of the X-Men?
>
> (Edens 1993/2009)

Startled by the offer of reintegration into the group, Morph begins to remember all of what happened to him. He confronts Mr. Sinister, who laughs and belittles him. Furious at how he has been corrupted and changed by Mr. Sinister, Morph helps the X-Men to defeat him, causing Mr. Sinister to flee along with the rest of his lackeys. The X-Men gather themselves together, only to see Morph leaving too.

> Wolverine: Morph! No! Come back!
>
> Beast: Let him go, Wolverine. Morph may be afraid of what he might do if he stays with us. He needs to learn to deal with what he has become.
>
> Wolverine: My friend . . . He was the only one who could ever make me laugh. I'm not going to desert him this time.
>
> (Edens 1993/2009)

The viewer knows that Wolverine is sincere and that Morph would be welcomed back into the X-Men should he decide to return. The story, however, has explored a quite murky situation involving the group not returning to save one of its own, and the resultant guilt and damage caused by this. The child viewer needs to make up his or her own mind whether Cyclops's decision to mount a strategic retreat was morally justified, or whether the group should have returned in an attempt to save him, even though they would have most likely been killed themselves. The story seems almost like a version of Kohlberg's moral dilemma about the marines in Korea (Kohlberg, cited by Duska and Whelan 1977: 122–123) and whether the group should escape at the expense of one of its members who has to stay behind (see Chapter 4) – but with the important and valuable addition that the consequences and aftermath of the moral decision that is made are also explored. There are no easy or falsely reassuring choices available, but the child viewer's moral reasoning has certainly been exercised.

Promoting and developing children's co-operation and empathy through superhero and conflict play

There are many ways that teachers and early years practitioners can utilize superhero and conflict play to develop children's co-operation, teamwork and understanding of other people's feelings and needs (not least through giving opportunities for children to engage with the kind of narratives discussed above). The examples that follow are indicative rather than exhaustive, and aim to illustrate something of the range of possibilities available.

The communal project

One West Sussex Reception class recently involved all its children in a series of linked 'Spider-Man' activities. Underpinning these were the staff's observations of several children's consistent and frequently expressed interest in Spider-Man and their associated spontaneous play. This interest became verbalized too:

> During our Topic on Ourselves the children talked about their favourite T.V. programmes and cartoons. Our . . . youngest boys just love Spider-man! They got so excited talking about it that they set all the others off and we decided to turn our home corner into Spider-man's cave!
>
> ('Superheroes in the Classroom: Spiderman Fun!'
> Display book for parents, 2008)

The staff were determined to build on and utilize the children's interest – something that is widely regarded as good practice, of course. The children were all involved in what became a large-scale collaborative project centring around the creation and use of a big role-play area. They were involved in the communal painting of a massive Spider-Man picture and in the choice of materials and artefacts that were used to create the area, including spider-web material and eight-legged model spiders that they made together. Other shared activities linked to Spider-Man took place too, such as lots of games involving counting up to 8 (such as finding eight things to fill up 'spider-web' bags), and singing songs:

> One elephant went out to play
> Using a Spider's web one day

He had such enormous fun
So he called for another elephant to come!

Being a Spider
Is such a lot of fun!
Hanging from the ceiling
And going for a run!
Being a Spider
Is absolutely great!
I've got more legs than anyone
'Cos I've got eight!

As well as the children's own role-play in the area, adult-initiated group games were played too:

HELP!
Eight naughty spiders are hiding in Spiderman's cave.
Can you help him to find them?

Phonics and letter work were linked to Spider-Man (for example, children had to explore words beginning with 'S' through a version of the game 'I Spy' and form simple consonant–vowel–consonant words from letter-cubes – something that would 'help' the many Spider-Man toys and action figures brought in by the children in their mission). Drawing and mathematical activities were also connected to Spider-Man (for example, through number-bond work involving adding more legs to pictures of spiders to make eight).

It can be seen that the staff of this Reception class were very imaginative in the way they connected up learning activities to the theme of Spider-Man, and that having this overarching theme helped unify both the range of activities on offer and the cohesion of the group, who felt like they were playing one big extended game together:

It was such a fun project and really grasped the children's imagination, so much so that they are full of ideas as to what we turn our corner into next.

('Superheroes in the Classroom: Spiderman Fun!'
Display book for parents, 2008)

The 'Superhero School'

In the spring of 2012 the Key Stage One department of a different West Sussex primary school decided to involve its children in a 'Superhero School' which ran for 6 weeks. This involved putting children in the role of 'learner superheroes' – taking its cue from some actual superhero groups, such as the X-Men, who start off by being students who are educated and mentored by Professor X in his 'School for Gifted Youngsters', and the Incredibles, the film of which involves the two children of the family receiving what amounts to a crash course in becoming superheroes. As learner superheroes, children were involved in play and decisions about what the proper expectations of super-heroes were; in other words, what types of behaviour and moral attitude should be demonstrated. The plan for the experience clearly demonstrates this:

> Rationale: Topic addresses a common interest – Superheroes – and encourages children to become *fit, healthy, kind and responsible – essential qualities of all superheroes.*
> (Year 1 Spring Term Superhero School Plan, 2012;
> emphasis added)

The discussions that took place as the experience developed involved issues such as how children who seemed upset or lonely in any particular situation (for example, excluded from games in the playground) might feel and ways of helping and offering friendship to them, the importance of politeness and the effects of both good and poor manners on others, and the requirement to stand up to any bullying and work against it. An emphasis was put not only on children behaving well themselves, but also particularly on the importance of modelling good behaviour to other children in the school and treating others well. The whole project was centred around a set of communal moral values:

> Values to be developed:
> Bronze – To know what is right & wrong.
> Silver – To understand the reasons for being honest and trustworthy.
> Gold – To strive to be honest and trustworthy.
> (Year 1 Spring Term Superhero School Plan, 2012)

A key feature of the Superhero School was a 'superhero den' role-play area and accompanying role-play activities. This superhero den was stocked with superhero gadgets (made by the children), phones and writing materials, 'mission cards' (each of which suggested a superhero mission that could be played out, and lots of superhero costumes, which, significantly, included costumes of teams of superheroes (the Fantastic Four and the Incredibles in particular) to encourage children to play and create superhero narratives together:

Me: What kind of activities did the children do?
Student teacher: They all worked in groups of three or four and they were
      each given a mission card, which might have been to rescue a cat out

of a tree or to save people from a burning building or something like that. And then what they would do is they then had to work together and say, 'Right, how can I use my superhero, and how can we use our traits to rescue that cat out of the tree, and who are we going to call on, and how can we all help each other?' They thought about what the problem was and what the solution was, and thought about how that hero could use his traits to sort the situation out, you know, and if you've got a mission that you need a team you can pull on each other's strengths.

At the end of the project the children's achievements were celebrated in a special event, as described by the student teacher:

> They all came together into one classroom and they were told how hard they'd worked and talked about what they had enjoyed about the topic and how might they improve upon it next time . . . And then they had a video from Spider-Man telling them how hard they'd worked, well done, they were now superheroes and had graduated from Superhero School. And they all got very excited!

The whole project treated the children as a unified group, each of whom had responsibilities towards the other members, but also a delight in them too. Working together and working towards the good of others were emphasized throughout the experience.

A variation on this approach took place in a Year 2/3 class in a smaller school situated elsewhere in West Sussex, also in the spring of 2012. After some preliminary work on superheroes the previous week (discussed further in Chapter 7), the class were informed that they were now going to transform into superhero versions of themselves, and that they would henceforth be known as the 'Superfriends'. Rather than generating a 'superhero charter' that contained a range of golden rules, each group of children was given one of several blank award certificates, each of which pictured one specific superhero and focused on a particular virtue associated with that superhero. Each group of children had to discuss what types of behaviour children in the school could show to deserve to be given their certificate, then record their ideas under the heading 'How to earn this award'. Here are some indicative examples of these awards:

The X-Men Award for Teamwork
The Wonder Woman Award for Showing How to be Good
The Catwoman Award for Looking After Animals
The Wolverine Award for Not Giving Up
The Spider-Girl Award for Helping Your Parents

The Hulk Award for Not Losing Your Temper
The Invisible Woman Award for Being a Good Friend
The Professor X Award for Keeping the Peace
The Batman Award for Determination

The groups shared their ideas once they had finished discussing and recording them, and the class were given the directive to earn as many of these awards as possible over the subsequent 2 weeks (which led to the end of the half-term) by demonstrating the appropriate behaviour. Here is an example of what they came up with:

The X-Men Award for Teamwork: How to Earn this Award:

Protect people in your team
Keep everybody safe
Be supportive to other people
Share your ideas with others
Listen to other people's ideas
Trust everyone in your team
Work together

As well as demonstrating such behaviour in their own class, one way these children could earn the awards was to model the desired behaviour while acting as learning-buddies to children in the Reception/Year 1 class, and also to show and explain the various award certificates to them – in other words, to act as moral exemplars and 'knowledgeable others' for the younger children. These younger children were very intrigued by this and (through a led discussion with the teacher) came up with their own award criteria:

The Spider-Girl Award for Helping Your Parents: How to Earn this Award:

Help to tidy up
Help collect food when it is ready
Look after your sisters and brothers
Help them play games nicely

The whole exercise revolved around the very superheroic dynamic of helping other people and taking some responsibility for their well-being and happiness. The project was regarded as a success by the teachers involved – not least because the messages about behaviour and responsibility towards others were explored through an area that was of great interest to the children themselves.

Story-telling, story-writing and drama

Ways of involving children in superhero story composition and drama are, perhaps, unlimited (and some will be discussed further later in this book), but here is an example of a drama activity firmly related to the development of teamwork, co-operation and empathy that was undertaken by the Year 2/3 children referred to above.

The drama activity took place once the Year 2/3 children had individually designed, drawn and described superhero versions of themselves and shared these with other children around their table. The children then moved into the school hall and were asked to get into groups (the groups being the people who had shared their superhero designs with each other). Each group of children was now told that they were a team that consisted of the superheroes that they had just created, and a few drama warm-up exercises took place which involved each team adopting suitable superhero poses, swooping through the night sky together, readying themselves for battle and answering phone calls from the police commissioner.

The teacher then set the scene for a loose narrative that involved these superhero teams trying to find and then rescue some people who were trapped somewhere, and suggested that a series of obstacles lay between the superheroes and the accomplishment of this objective. The children were invited to flesh out the detail of these obstacles and narrative and share their ideas with the whole class. The teacher then used these ideas to narrate a developing story based around the children searching for clues, finding ways into the building, disabling traps, and so on. This story was acted out in small steps by the children while it was being narrated. Each group of children had to agree ways of using a combination of all of their superhero powers to get through force-fields, fly over high barriers, stay on the right route, deal with suddenly emerging problems, pick up and carry people being rescued and other such tasks. The successful development of the drama depended upon all the children in any group agreeing on each team member's role during each step of the narrative and how each scene would be played as a unified whole; in other words, they had to act as a coherent team as well as portray one. The teacher also encouraged the children to think about how the various characters (whether superheroes, villains or people who needed rescuing) might feel at different times in the story and portray these feelings in their drama – something that the children duly did, resulting in emotions such as fear, worry, determination, happiness and frustration being expressed in character.

A simple extension to this activity could involve groups of children being given differentiated writing-frames, possibly in the form of comic-book panels on A3 sheets of paper. As a suggestion, the simplest writing-frame could consist of four panels, a more sophisticated one of six, and, with older children, the most sophisticated being a two-page writing-frame consisting of 12 panels overall. Each panel could include a very short synopsis of the key action to be represented in it, as illustrated below:

We meet the superheroes.	The problem or threat is introduced.
We meet the villains.	Confrontation between the superheroes and the villains.
The threat is overcome and the villains are defeated.	A happy ending – or is it? A link is made to the next thrilling adventure!

Children could individually design their own superheroes before this activity, and combine them in groups through drama activities such as that reported above. Now they could work in groups to compose stories involving their home-grown superheroes. The teacher could encourage the children to ensure that each superhero gets properly represented in every group story, and remind them that they would be expected to agree on the plot-line and overall composition of the story, the words to be used, which children would be responsible for drawing or writing particular parts of the story, and so on, something that would involve a high degree of co-operation and task-sharing.

Higher-ability children could be given more complex and nuanced story-panels representing even more challenging and sophisticated tasks:

One superhero gets duped by the villains and joins them.	The duped superhero leads the others into a trap.
The superheroes break out of the trap.	The duped superhero realizes he or she was wrong. The group take him or her back.

Children would have to decide which of their superheroes would get fooled, tempted or otherwise misled by the villains, and how. They would also need to identify what kind of argument or appeal the other superheroes in the group could use to bring their errant team member back to them. Teachers could support children engaged in this activity by asking them what potential weaknesses each of their superheroes might have and suggesting some possibilities (such as being quick to anger, jealous of other teammates' achievements, or prone to running into situations without thinking them through first). The children could try out different possibilities by dramatizing them and playing them out to see which ones they liked the best. The children would have to consider the emotional and moral characteristics of the superheroes that they were creating with some attention to detail for this to work well; in other words, this activity could have quite a lot of depth.

Overall, such an activity would require children not only to imagine how their fictional team of superheroes might relate to each other, and what emotions and loyalties might find themselves in play, but also to act as a unified and collaborative team themselves and work together successfully to produce a shared product that they all could have pride in and ownership of.

7 Superhero and conflict play and children's sense of self and self-worth

Introduction

The importance of nurturing children's security and understanding of self and belief in their own ability to succeed has been recognized in education for a very long time (and perhaps always by good teachers and parents – see Plato 2007). This importance is reflected officially in the EYFS (Department for Education (DfE) 2012), which categorizes 'self-confidence and self-awareness' together as being one of the key strands of personal, social and emotional development (PSED), which is itself one of the three Prime Areas of Learning and Development. The aspiration is that PSED will help enable children 'to develop a positive sense of themselves, and others' (DfE 2012: 6). The current National Curriculum (Department for Education and Employment (DfEE) and Qualifications and Curriculum Authority (QCA) 1999) also recognizes the importance of nurturing and informing children's security and understanding of self, stating that children should be enabled to 'recognise their own worth . . . and understand how they are developing personally and socially, tackling many of the spiritual, moral, social and cultural issues that are part of growing up' (DfEE and QCA 1999: 136).

Recognizing one's own worth requires a sound understanding of oneself and a confident, positive and realistic appreciation of the potential that might be there to achieve, overcome difficulties and be a person of value, whether academically, socially, creatively, or morally. This chapter will explore some key understandings of how children develop a sense of identity and self-worth, how they might express ideas about identity in creative ways, and how engagement with superhero play and superhero narratives might support and exercise these things.

The development of self-concept and self-esteem

Children do not exist in isolation. Their earliest concepts and feelings about identity emanate from the relationships they find themselves a part of – particularly the attachment relationship they have with their parents, closely followed by other significant attachments to other family members. Such relationships are profound in their impact on children's well-being and development; indeed, Bowlby (1953/1965: 13) went so far as to say:

> What is believed to be essential for mental health is that the infant and young child should experience a warm, intimate and continuous relationship with [his or her] mother or permanent mother substitute . . . in which both find satisfaction and enjoyment.

The word 'essential' was not chosen lightly: virtually all researchers in this field have agreed that children thrive when the attachment bond shared between them and their primary attachment figures is demonstrably loving, accepting and consistent. For example, according to Adamson (2008: 3): 'Neuroscientific research is demonstrating that loving, stable, secure, stimulating and rewarding relationships with family and caregivers in the earliest months and years of life are critical for almost all aspects of a child's development.'

Whatever the qualities and characteristics of the attachment bonds are, it seems that children form what Bowlby (1969: 236) termed an 'internal working model' of their attachment relationships; in other words, they carry in their heads ideas and beliefs about how they are perceived, treated and valued by their primary attachment figures (and all their other attachment figures, such as siblings or grandparents). These ideas and beliefs have a direct impact on children's concepts of themselves – a significant factor in their internal working models of their identities is the way they believe the significant people in their lives see them. Woolford (2007: 85) identifies two distinct but related aspects of this internal working model of self as follows:

Self-concept: Individuals' knowledge and beliefs about themselves – their ideas, feelings, attitudes and expectations.
Self-esteem: The value each of us places on our own characteristics, abilities and behaviour.

What this all demonstrates is that if children receive consistent messages (whether verbally or physically) that they are loved and of value, for example, then they are much more likely to believe that they are deserving of being loved and that they do have some intrinsic value than if they receive messages that are either mixed in their content or suggest that they are just a nuisance or difficulty, or even that they are actively disliked or found worthless.

As children develop their socialization (for example, by attending nursery or school), then equivalent internal working models are formed of the relationships that are experienced in these social contexts, including the relationships with teachers and early years professionals. In addition, as Mitchell and Ziegler (2007) note, children whose concept of self-worth is informed through positive and loving messages from their parents and caregivers are more likely to be popular among their peers at school than those who have not received such messages, probably because their own capacity to build positive and mutually valuing relationships with other people is informed by their own early experiences of such things with their parents. All of this is why a common element of good early years and educational practice is the explicit support given to the establishment and development of children's positive self-esteem by (hopefully) all professionals whom children meet during their education.

The importance of self-esteem and self-actualization

The level of self-worth (or self-esteem) that children develop can have a profound effect on the well-being, happiness and success that they achieve as they mature and grow. An important milestone in the recognition of this came in the form of Abraham Maslow's 'A Theory of Human Motivation'. Maslow's (1943: 374) essential proposition was as follows:

> There are at least five sets of goals, which we may call basic needs. These are briefly physiological, safety, love, esteem and self-actualization. In addition, we are motivated by the desire to achieve or maintain the various conditions upon which these basic satisfactions rest and by certain more intellectual desires. . . . man is a perpetually wanting animal.

Maslow (1943, 1962) suggested that these five 'basic needs' need to be met in a certain order, and that the best chance of attaining happiness and self-fulfilment came from satisfaction of all five of them. To start with, people require the things that sustain life (oxygen, good nutrition, warmth, and so on). Then they need to feel safe and without threat to their lives. Once these crucial things are established, according to Maslow, the key need is for love, shown through good nurture, recognition and acceptance, delight in one's company, and the explicit demonstration of affection; in fact, all the things that Bowlby (1953/1965, 1969) considered essential for children's emotional well-being and growth – and which are probably essential for adults' emotional well-being too (Oatley et al. 2006).

The next two needs in this hierarchy are strongly related to each other. 'Esteem' for Maslow meant self-esteem; the need is for one's own valuing of oneself and faith in one's own worth, potential for achievement, and ability to successfully deal with any difficulties or setbacks that might arise. Maslow insisted that without such confidence and belief in oneself one could never be truly happy or fulfilled, as whatever situation in life was attained, there would be too much self-doubt to allow people to enjoy it or believe in its security or that any good situation in life was actually deserved.

Even so, according to Maslow, the existence of high self-esteem is not enough to facilitate happiness and well-being in itself. What is needed is 'self-actualization' (Maslow 1943: 374), which is really having and utilizing the opportunity to be the person one considers oneself to be in practice – in other words, if a person considers himself or herself to be creative, that he or she has the opportunity to create (and, ideally, have his or her creations valued by others); if a woman considers herself to be a good mother, that she has the opportunity to be a good mother in practice; if a person considers himself or herself to be brave, then he or she has the opportunity to show bravery to the world, rather than just keep it as a private mental idea about himself or herself. Dweck (2000: 128) puts it as follows: self-actualization 'is how you feel when you are striving wholeheartedly for worthwhile things; it's how you experience yourself when you are using your abilities to the fullest in the service of what you deeply value'.

None of this happens in a vacuum, however, as further exploration of the examples above will demonstrate. A person who regards himself or herself to be a creative person will first of all need to have developed ideas about what being a creative person is; similarly, a woman who aspires to be a good mother will need to have developed a mental model of what qualities and characteristics such a mother has, and a person who regards himself or herself as brave will need to have been exposed to models of behaviour and attitude that signify bravery or its absence. In other words, all such ideas about oneself are informed by all the *role models* of creative and not so creative people, good and not so good mothers, brave and not so brave figures (and, indeed any other attributes of character or behaviour that are valued) that children are exposed to. This includes fictional role models too, and, indeed, all the stories that children engage with which explore the qualities of character and behaviour considered valuable or significant.

Superheroes and children's self-actualization

This is where superheroes come in. Superheroes are nothing if not bold, confident and dynamic role models of self-actualization. Superheroes present themselves as people who are capable, powerful, definite, confident, and, most significantly for children, *what they mean to be*. Superman, the most powerful superhero of all (and the default template for all the superheroes who follow), is probably the most obvious example: his exaggerated physique, boldly coloured costume, square jaw, deep voice, and, of course, his superpowers mark him out as kind of modern-day Samson, and certainly as a definite and obvious hero in the classical tradition. Just as telling as his physical prowess and appearance, however, is his manner: he is courteous, kind, well spoken, considerate, noble, and dedicated – both to the welfare of the world and the woman whom he loves. Not only that, but he looks villains squarely in the eye; he is not daunted or intimidated by them, nor will he stand by and let their evildoing or mischief continue without attempting to stop it. In other words, he presents himself *how he is*: his morality, character and mission all find bold, clear and confident expression; his primary-coloured costume and powerful, open stance say 'Here I am, I am a definite and capable presence in the world, I exist, and I am not afraid of you'.

All superheroes have something of these qualities. They present themselves to the world with huge visible expression of their character and super-identity: Spider-Man is dressed in a costume covered with spider-web patterns and swings on spider-webs; Catwoman dresses in a cat-suit and moves in a feline manner; Captain America is dressed in American stars and stripes and uses a shield which symbolizes his mission to protect; Batman wears a bat's pointed ears and a bat-wing-like cape and is shrouded in a dark costume that emulates the night-time when bats come out. Superheroes present themselves as larger-than-life figures wrapped in costumes and symbols, and using language and names, that signify who they are and what they stand for – such as the 'Lantern' part of Green Lantern's name and costume, which stands for the light of truth and for the mission of all the Green Lanterns (there is one for each inhabited sector of the universe) to reveal and combat evil:

> In brightest day, in darkest night
> No evil shall escape my sight
> Let those who worship evil's might
> Beware my power: Green Lantern's light!

(Burnett 2011)

This overt confidence and definite expression of identity offered by superhero role models can be deeply appealing to children; they can dress up as Spider-Man, Superman or Wonder Woman and suddenly be bold, heroic, brave, confident and superpowered as a result. Playing in the guise of such characters allows children to self-actualize and express themselves as confident individuals who make a difference and have an impact upon the world. It also allows them to explore *possibility*: if they can imagine something, however fantastical, then the device of having superpowers enables this imagined possibility to find expression – often in very creative ways. Fly to the moon to find the treasure? Why not? Turn invisible to remain hidden from the guards?

Go ahead! Grow taller on telescopic legs to see over the building? Quite logical! It is not that children will literally believe that they are capable of such things in real life; it is, rather, that they can explore what it might be like to be that kind of person and explore which elements of that kind of person's character (such as confidence, or moral determination, or fearlessness, or ability to come up with a solution) they might recognize in or desire for themselves – just as children playing being mothers do not really believe that they are mothers in real life, but are still trying out and finding expression for the actual mothering instincts that might be in their nature and part of their identity.

In other words, children's superhero play (in common with much other role play) sees children exploring *possibilities of self* through their adoption of different personas and roles in play and story creation – and these *possible* selves inform and contribute to the development of children's *actual* selves, as children explore possibilities of self that they find desirable – and also, sometimes, possibilities of self that they worry might come true (see Engel 1999) – such as the Hulk's uncontrollable aggression or Batman's deep emotional loneliness (see Chapter 10).

Superheroes are not just defined by their grand-scale powers and costumes, though, but also by their identities as recognizably *human* people with particular personalities, moral standpoints and individual character traits, and children exploring superhero personas have these things role-modelled to them too. Nowhere is this more apparent than in superheroes' everyday-life identities. Superman, for example, is not just an almost all-powerful Kryptonian demigod, he is also the mild-mannered Clark Kent, who is awkward, bespectacled, and, though a very good reporter, is seen as a bit of a weakling by many of those around him; Spider-Man is really the deeply intelligent and scientific, but insecure and rather nerdy, teenager Peter Parker, who gets picked on by the jock Flash Thompson; Batman, whose super-hero self deals with the darkest and most disturbing aspects of humanity, is also the billionaire Bruce Wayne, who presents himself as a useless, frivolous and irrelevant playboy much of the time. Such aspects of superheroes' non-super-identities can be significant to children too, as can be seen from Matthew Stadlen's interview with the radio and television reporter John Humphrys (BBC News 2011):

Stadlen: How did you get into journalism?
Humphrys: I read as a little boy *Superman* comics, you know. That was after the war . . . Superman, Clark Kent in his day job, was, of course a journalist, a reporter, and I figured in my 5- or 6-year-old brain, become a reporter and, you know, you become Superman, and beautiful women like Lois Lane fancy you, and that's how it worked in my very childish brain, but it stuck, and I never wanted to be anything else other than a reporter.

It is very significant that the caring, capable, and moral aspects of superhero characters are what define them, regardless of the way other characters understand them, or of the personas that their non-super-identities seem to demonstrate. Superheroes' innate heroism and moral character always come through, regardless of the situation they are in, or whether they are in or out of costume. There are plenty of stories where superheroes suffer some situation that means they temporarily lose their superpowers, but they proceed with their mission anyway and wade into danger to accomplish some good, because that is who they are. Such stories demonstrate that it is not their *powers* that define superheroes as heroes and good people, it is their *character*, moral integrity, and willingness to act on their moral principles in order to promote good and overcome evil.

In other words, the moral, admirable and heroic aspects of superheroes can be genuinely emulated by real human children too, even if their powers cannot. (It is interesting that many superheroes have had less powerful children or teenagers as partners or sidekicks, such as Captain America's Bucky, Flash's Kid Flash, Wonder Woman's younger sister Wonder Girl, Green Arrow's Speedy, Superman's younger cousin Supergirl, and, most famously, Batman's Robin; and most stories involving such characters have revolved around the dynamic of the child learning some important moral or emotional message from the adult.)

Superheroes' dualism of identity can be a great source of interest for children, especially as it explores the exact issue that lies behind children's judgement of self-worth – the relationship between their own actual selves and the way their selves are perceived and valued (or not valued) by the external world. Clark Kent, for example, might be belittled, slighted or ignored by people around him, but inside he is really the capable and confident Superman; similarly, Peter Parker might be teased or bullied by his rather more stupid and ignorant classmates, but he is really Spider-Man and can run rings around them. In other words, imagining a superhero persona for oneself might be a very attractive way for a child to deal with any negative or destructive messages received from the outside world about aspects of his or her self. As Engel (1999: 44) puts it: 'Everyone, in telling the story of his own life, casts himself as either the conquering or the suffering hero . . . Even young children depict themselves as some kind of hero.'

To be the 'conquering hero' is to be self-actualized. To be the 'suffering hero' is to still have all the valuable and worthy attributes of a hero, even if these remain unrecognized or dismissed by the surrounding world. Either way, the child remains strong and has self-worth; the conceit of imagining oneself as a superhero invests the child with an imaginative framework for holding one's head up to the outside world, as this recollection from a teacher demonstrates:

> My eyesight really began to get bad around the age of 11, and I had to wear these very unflattering National Health Service specs, and lots of

children in my new class teased me about them and called me 'Four-eyes' and 'Softy Walter' from the *Beano* and so on. But one of the things that really helped, I remember, was that I was an avid comics reader and I loved Superman, and I would pretend that my glasses-wearing was just a disguise like Clark Kent's, and that meanwhile I could use my X-ray vision to see these other children's rather mean characters for what they were, and that I was powerful like Superman really, just biding my time in my secret identity and not giving it away. And that really helped.

Some superheroes, of course, do not have a secret identity; rather, their identities are there for all the world to see. Reed Richards and his family and best friend are known to be the Fantastic Four; Oliver Queen is publicly the Green Arrow; Aquaman simply *is* the King of Atlantis. These superheroes role-model a valuable 'take-me-or-leave-me' approach to their identity: they are who they are, they are confident and definite about declaring their identities, and they will remain who they are regardless of what the outside world feels about it. This overt self-assurance can also act as a very positive role model of being proud and confident in oneself.

Indeed, children's superhero play does not always involve them pretending to be pre-existing superheroes and other people such as Batman or Spider-Man, but it can also involve them in creating and playing as their own made-up superheroes as an explicit and confident form of self-expression. In this situation children's ideas about their own actual identify can be represented as aspects of the superheroes that they create. One Year 1 girl in a school in Hove, for example, was very fond of dancing in real life and was often involved in dancing activity: the superhero she created (during a class literacy project on superheroes) was called 'Super Dancing Girl'. Another girl in the same class who enjoyed sports and PE described her superhero creation ('Fieer Woomon') as follows:

> She can run rily frast and can scip rily very farst.

Similarly, in a Reception/Year 1 class in a West Sussex school, a girl who was very fond of her long hair as a strong and attractive feature of her identity created a female superhero who was drawn with very long blonde hair and whose power was 'My hair strech'.

It is not a new idea that children's play can contribute towards their representation of ideas about self (see Lowenfield 1967), and these examples do seem to suggest that children's self-actualization will find expression during play. Superhero play, with its strong and definite role models of self-actualization, does appear to be a very potent vehicle for encouraging children's self-actualization, especially as the limitless possibilities opened up by the device of having superpowers allow children to explore ideas about self that are beyond the literal.

Superheroes and children's identity as members of humanity

We have seen how children's understanding of self is not limited to actual, personal experience and the way one's actual self seems to be regarded by others in real life; it is also informed by consideration of the whole range of possible role models and exemplars offered by society and culture, and children's exploration of *possibilities of self* through their adoption of different personas and roles in play and story creation.

Similarly, children's identity is not static. Children do not just go through a process of discovering and identifying characteristics of their identity as if it was a single, unchanging thing to be revealed; they actively try out possibilities for their own identity to see how well they seem to fit their developing concepts of self. Much of this process is in response to children's observations of role models and their behaviour and lives, and it seems that such observations are *storyfied*; in other words, children contextualize their observations and experiences into unfolding stories about their own selves and how they relate to the world and the people in it. MacIntyre (1981: 216) puts it this way: 'I can only answer the question "What am I to do?" if I can answer the prior question "Of what story or stories do I find myself a part?"'

Some of the stories that surround the child are personal and environmental; the story might be that the child is part of such-and-such a family, which operates physically, socially and emotionally in such-and-such a way and is situated in such-and-such an environment. Some of the stories, however, relate to cultural ideas of self and possibility (and, indeed, humanity) that are much larger in their scale. Authors such as Campbell (1949/1993), Bruner (1962/1979) and Bettleheim (1976) point to the impact that grander and more symbolic cultural narratives (particularly myths and fairy tales) can have in children's developing identity, sense of self, and desire for the future evolution and actualization of self. Bruner (1962/1979: 38) goes so far as to say: 'Myth becomes the tutor, the shaper of identities. It is here that personality imitates myth.'

The archetypes of human character available in myth, according to Campbell (1949/1993) and Bruner (1962/1979), give us our key examples of what it is to be a man or woman, and we relate our daily existence to these larger-than-life figures and their narratives in an attempt to understand our situation and identity as human beings, and gain an idea of direction and purpose (and possibly destiny). As Campbell (1949/1993: 19–25) puts it: 'In myth, the problems and solutions shown are valid for all mankind. . . . The heroes of all time have gone before us: the labyrinth is thoroughly known; we have only to follow the thread of the hero-path.' In other words, the world's fantastical and archetypal stories involving quests, monsters and heroes cannot just be classed as amusing fantasies that while away the hours pleasantly; rather, they serve to instruct us about human nature, human emotion and moral choice. Their heroes and the dilemmas they face instruct us about morality, love and character: Hercules struggles with his labours, but does not give up; Zeus confronts his father, Cronus; Icarus flies too far above his proper status as a human being and too near to godhood; men wage war over Helen; Midas makes the mistake of loving gold too much; Orpheus attempts to rescue his wife from death in the Underworld, and so on.

Once again, this is where superheroes come in. Superhero characters and themes exist on a grand, mythic scale. The narratives superheroes immerse themselves in are full of myth-like large and powerful themes – destiny, justice, sacrifice, love, brotherhood and mission, to name but a few – and their stories give accessible expression to deep ideas about the nature of life and what it is to be human. Sometimes the scale of events is huge, with the whole world, if not the universe, under threat, and sometimes it is small and intimate; but there is always some universal consideration of the human condition and of human destiny and potential being explored. Consider these two examples, both large-scale, but one much more intimate too.

The first comes from the famous 'Galactus Trilogy' (1966–1967, and the basis for the *Fantastic Four: Rise of the Silver Surfer* film of 2007), in which the world comes under threat from Galactus, an all-powerful god-like being of such a scale that he consumes whole planets just to stay alive. Galactus first dismisses human beings as being beneath his notice, like insignificant insects, but the actions and determination of the Fantastic Four, along with the moral arguments put by the Watcher and the rebellion of his herald, the Silver Surfer (prompted by the compassion shown by Susan Storm, the Invisible Woman and Alicia, the Thing's blind girlfriend) cause him to eventually – and reluctantly – revise his judgement:

> At last I perceive the glint of *glory* within the race of *man*! Be ever *worthy* of that glory, humans . . . be ever mindful of your promise of greatness! For it shall one day lift you beyond the stars . . . or bury you within the ruins of war!! *The choice is yours!!*
>
> (Lee 1967: 10)

The second example comes from *Kingdom Come*, a story set in an undefined period of years in the future. The Spectre arrives on Earth and, angel-like, appears to the elderly Pastor Norman McCay in the night:

> The Spectre: I have *need* of you, Norman McCay.
> McCay: And now the visions talk to me. I have gone mad . . .

The Spectre: Hardly. In fact, your *sanity* may be *paramount* to mankind's survival. Even as I stand *before* you, an act of *unspeakable evil* has begun to manifest. *Armageddon* is *fast approaching*. But you *know* this. You have the *dreams*.

McCay: You . . . see into my *mind* . . . my *soul*? You are an *angel* . . .?

The Spectre: Of a sort. A *higher power* has charged me with the task of *punishing* those *responsible* for this coming evil. Long ago I would have judged *swiftly*, with *clarity* . . . but my *faculties* are not what they *once were*. In order to *carry out* my task, I must *anchor* myself to a human soul who seeks *justice*.

McCay: But I don't . . .

The Spectre: You *will*.

(Waid and Ross 2008: 29)

The story sets itself up on a huge scale, as the extract above demonstrates; in fact, it is akin to a version of the Book of Revelation (which is referred to throughout) in the largeness of the events it portrays. The human soul the Spectre anchors himself too, however, is Norman McCay's, and the whole story that follows is seen through McCay's eyes and subject to his judgement. The moral standpoint of the story, in other words, comes not from any of the many superheroes who appear within it (though they certainly inform it), but from the moral perspective of an ordinary, non-superpowered human being.

The story starts with the reintroduction of the now-retired Superman, who is portrayed as a dispirited, disillusioned recluse from the world, hiding behind a beard and ponytail, and who devotes all his energy to keeping his parents' farm going, simply because it was his parents' farm, and is now almost his only emotional link to the rest of the world:

The Spectre: You know him by a name he has not used in *ten years* . . .

McCay: Superman . . .

The Spectre: Not since his self-imposed *exile*.

McCay: My *God* . . . he is so *alone*.

The Spectre: Not always.

Wonder Woman: Hello, Clark . . . *Kal*.

Superman: Diana, haven't seen you in *months*. What brings you to the *farm*?

Wonder Woman: The vain hope that you're not still *here*.

Superman: These are my *roots*.

Wonder Woman: You can't live *forever* in solitude.

Superman: I'm *Superman*. I can do *anything*.

Wonder Woman: Except, apparently, face your *fear* . . . Kal, you've lost *so much* since I first met you.

Superman: Earthlings *die. You* know that.

Wonder Woman: They were your *parents,* Cla . . . *Kal.* And *she* was your *wife. Don't* call them *Earthlings.* Here me *out.* I –

Superman: I have *work* to do, Diana. *Here,* things *grow.*

(Waid and Ross 2008: 32–33)

As well as the large-scale themes of justice, retribution and punishment that *Kingdom Come* contains, it also very movingly puts forward the story of a broken and defeated man (Superman) and how he regains his sense of purpose, usefulness, and – possibly most importantly – *hope.* It shows that a man can be blessed with almost unimaginable power, but still remain a man who can suffer and be defeated by guilt, grief and disillusionment. It follows him as he is supported by his friends and recovers his sense of self and ability to make a difference to the world, and it ends with the most classic symbol of hope for the future – he is to become a father and nurture a new child into the world. One of its key themes is that every single person matters and makes a difference, even in the face of more powerful people and events that are vast and seemingly beyond any single individual's ability to affect.

This, above all, is the key message that superheroes offer children about self: self *matters* and is *valuable,* and people's individual moral choices and attachments to each other make all the difference in the world. Engaging with the mythic storylines and themes and the large-scale characters that are superheroes does not make children feel small, ordinary or merely human; rather, it allows them to be part of all existence and all the overarching themes that are greater than themselves, and feel that they, too, can be morally strong, capable, valuable and able to make a difference to the world. It does not matter that they are not grown-up or superpowered or perfect (as the Ancient One explains to Dr. Strange, he was chosen 'to continue the care of mankind' because 'Our order does not desire placid seekers of truth. We desire men with flaws' (Englehart 1973: 33)). They follow the hero-path laid out before them because they have the capability and potential to be heroes too.

8 The moral themes that lie behind superhero and conflict play

Introduction

> Me: So, who likes superheroes?
> [*The entire Year 4/5 class put their hands up.*]
> Me: Wow! Okay, why do you like them?
> Two children simultaneously: Because they save people.
> [*Everyone else nods or says 'Yeah'*]

As discussed in Chapter 4, children's moral development involves their development of moral values, their development of moral reasoning, and the resultant intertwining of the two. Many situations and scenarios that children may encounter in real life and in the stories they absorb are likely to stimulate thinking and feeling about what have been commonly recognized (see Law 2007) as key moral issues and themes, namely:

What is right (or good) and what is wrong (or evil), and how do they differ?
What constitutes being a good person, and why should one be such a person?
What is the aim of goodness?
How should good and evil acts be responded to?

While all good culture explores these issues (and more), superhero characters and narratives are particular in that their very existence is centred around them. Superheroes and their supervillain counterparts take particular and explicit – and often deeply felt – moral (or immoral) standpoints. Superhero stories are almost universally constituted so that the child reader or viewer knows what the good and most desirable outcome would be (for example, the rescue of the hostages, the prevention of death or damage, the retrieval of property, the removal of the threat, the reunion of the separated) and wishes this good outcome to be achieved. They are also structured so that the child reader or viewer can see the differences in character and motivation between the superheroes and their opponents. In other words, superhero narratives can be understood as expressions of what has been termed *classical dualism*.

Classical dualism

The basic notion of classical dualism – 'classical' because it found much expression in ancient Greek writers and thinkers, although it has also been expressed ever since in a variety of ways, including by Aquinas (1273) and Descartes (1596–1650) – is that our human situation is composed of dualities (for example, body–soul or body–mind, good–evil, and reason–emotion) and that part of the task of being human is to determine the relationship between the two parts of each duality and whether we should favour one part over the other. Pythagoras (570–495 BC), for example, considered that our souls are trapped in the physical shells of our bodies, and that the most profitable human actions were ones that advanced and nurtured the soul rather than the body.

Aristotle (384–322 BC) took the notion of dualism further. He considered that all behaviour should be directed towards a particular goal (or *telos*), which is the establishment of what is good: 'Every rational activity aims at some end or good . . . Hence the good has been rightly defined as "that at which all things aim"' (Aristotle 2004: 3). Aristotle held that every human being was a moral agent whose actions and decisions worked either towards the establishment of 'the good' or against it: the basic dualism at the heart of moral and ethical issues. Determining what 'the good' consists of, however, was another matter, and, for Aristotle, success in doing so depended on the exercise of rationality. The development of the ability to reason, along with the accumulation of life experience to give this reasoning some substance and context, and the effort to ensure one's own actions were in the service of the good, would give a person the best chance to 'reason well . . . in accordance with virtue' (Stokes 2003: 25) – which in some ways is very similar to Piaget's (1932/1965) and Kohlberg's (1984) thoughts on the matter – see Chapter 4. Aristotle's *Nichomachean Ethics* is full of dualisms which, he says, need to be resolved for the development of virtuous character and the establishment of the good: rationality versus irrationality, restraint versus licentiousness, selfishness versus generosity, pleasure versus the contemplative life, and so on.

Aristotle's approach to morality has been commonly termed *virtue ethics*, as it seeks to identify what character traits and types of behaviour are most virtuous – or, in other words, which are most likely to lead to 'the good' or be good in themselves. As Kohlberg (1984) and Piaget (1932/1965) demonstrated (see Chapter 4), much of children's moral development also consists of their attempts to identify such things. Virtues identified by Aristotle include wisdom, understanding, rationality, impartiality, prudence, temperance, patience, generosity and gratitude, among many others, while their dualistic opposites (such as selfishness, impatience and irrationality) are to be shunned. He sums up good conduct as being 'To feel or act towards the right person to the right extent at the right time for the right reason in the right way' (Aristotle 2004: 48). It can be suggested that the level of good judgement that is required to do this, especially in any consistent way, is vast – and Aristotle (2004: 48) himself adds 'that is not easy, and it is not everyone that can do it. Hence to do these well is a rare, laudable and fine achievement'.

What this demonstrates, among other things, is that Kohlberg's (1984) insistence that children's moral development is properly measured by their ability to *reason* which moral principles might apply and how they might apply in any given moral scenario is not a recent idea, but belongs in a tradition of thought about ethics and morality that is one of the most established in Western civilization. For both Aristotle and Kohlberg it is not enough just to be good (say, through one's own natural personality or unconscious habitual behaviour) but rather one has to have rational ownership and understanding of *why* some behaviour or character trait could be considered to be good.

Aristotle's approach to ethics also gave rise to the development of 'teleological ethics', which is the attempt to determine what the sought-after 'good' might be, whether 'happiness, equality, freedom, justice or some other prized social value' (Baker-Fletcher 2000: 22). This approach to ethics focuses strongly on the consequences and intended consequences of any action; in other words, on the motives behind and results of any behaviour or decision. As discussed in Chapter 4, Piaget (1932/1965) found that children typically prioritize the importance of the results of any action early on in their moral development, but that their subsequent ability to give a higher level of consideration to the motives for any action is a sign of a higher level of moral development (as seen earlier in the twin stories of Marie and Margaret).

It is this range of themes (the possible virtues or vices that determine whether one is of good or not so good character, the nature of the desired good, the motives that lie behind actions, and the consequences of actions) that superhero narratives seek to explore. As children move through such stories they are exposed to opportunities to ask moral questions and make moral judgements about whichever particular moral themes the individual stories contain. As Bruner (1990: 80) observed, 'logical propositions are most easily comprehended by the child when they are embedded in an ongoing story', and this applies to superhero stories as much as any others, with the 'logical propositions' being, perhaps, that justice should be pursued, or that the innocent should be protected, or that love is better than hate, or that people have moral duties towards one another. This chapter will now illustrate some ways in which this happens.

Being of good character

> Young children . . . are in the thick of being socialized. They are being taught what is right or wrong or good or bad. They are being schooled in the complex world of rules and expectations; what it means to be a good child and not a bad one. Many of the stories they're told teach about good guys and bad guys and what happens to them.
>
> (Dweck 2000: 96–97)

Superheroes are of inherently good character, and the stories that surround them show this good character at work, as will be seen. Most superheroes, however, do not spring out of the womb with their goodness fully established; more commonly, they go through an experience or set of experiences that cause them to rethink or discover their genuine moral attitudes or priorities. In addition, many superheroes have moments of doubt; they might wish to adopt a worthy moral position or behaviour, but worry about their own character flaws and failings and whether they are up to it. Typically, of course, their stories show that the truth of their character will out, in other words, that their inherent goodness will overcome their own doubts and any other obstacles that might come their way. Children absorbing such stories are faced with exemplars of the development and expression of good moral character, and also of what difficulties, temptations and blind alleys a person might face as he or she struggles to act with moral integrity. They are given role models of characters who demonstrate how moral issues might be responded to and how obstacles to being good and doing good things might be overcome.

One of the most famous examples of this is the origin story of Spider-Man (see Chapter 2). A reminder: the skinny, bespectacled Peter Parker, who is picked on by his classmates at college, suddenly gains 'spider-powers' through the bite of a radioactive spider. His first impulse is that he could use his new powers to make some money for himself and his beloved Aunt May and Uncle Ben – the only people who seem to care for him in the world. However, while earning money from showing off his spider-powers, Spider-Man allows a thief to run past him and escape on the grounds that it is nothing to do with him – that is, that he has no moral responsibility to stop the thief. Once Peter travels home, however, he discovers that his beloved Uncle Ben has been shot dead by the criminal whom he had let escape earlier. 'My fault! – All my fault!' sobs Peter, before the very first Spider-Man story ever published concludes: 'And a lean, silent figure fades slowly into the gathering darkness, aware at last that in this world with great power must also come great responsibility!' (Lee and Ditko 1962: 11). The trauma suffered over his uncle's murder, combined with the ever-present thought that he himself bears a great responsibility for this, completely alters Spider-Man's moral outlook – or, at least, corrects it to what it might have been had Peter Parker not felt aggrieved with a world that seemed to isolate and bully him.

This theme of a moral realization dawning and changing attitude and behaviour is something of a constant in superhero narratives, as can be seen by charting the similarities between two superhero origin stories, one written in 1963 and one in 2008. The earlier story concerns the origin of Dr. Strange (the 'Master of Black Magic'). This story starts with a desperate, unkempt, ragged man finally coming across the home of the Ancient One in India. He has searched for this Ancient One for some time for purely selfish and self-serving reasons – he wishes the Ancient One to restore him to his former rich and successful status in a materialistic world. The Ancient One is not so willing to oblige, however, and holds Stephen Strange motionless while he looks into his mind to determine the truth about him; which, of course, he narrates for the benefit of the child reader:

> You were proud, haughty, successful! But you cared little for your fellow men . . . Money . . . that was all that interested you . . . all you cared about . . . to you the problems of others were less than nothing!
>
> (Lee and Ditko 1963: 4–5)

Needless to say, as in many moral fables, the bubble bursts, and we hear that Stephen Strange suffered an accident that led to a reversal of fortune:

> Others tried to help you, but you were too bitter . . . too full of pent-up self-pity! And so you went into seclusion . . . you spent your days brooding, as bitterness filled your soul!
>
> (Lee and Ditko 1963: 5)

At this point, in flashback, we see Stephen Strange's own hubris at work:

> I must be the best . . . the greatest!!! Or else . . . *nothing*! I'll never consent to work for anyone else!
>
> (Lee and Ditko 1963: 5)

The child reader sees that Stephen Strange has been brought down greatly as a result of his own pride and self-importance, and his refusal of the help and care offered by others regardless of whether he deserved such things. The reader also sees the corrosive effects of self-importance and self-pity on the once powerful and arrogant man.

The Ancient One, of course, refuses to give Stephen Strange what he wants, but allows him a few days to stay and recuperate. Strange sulks, but has no choice. During these few days, however, he becomes aware of a diabolical betrayal being hatched by the Ancient One's erstwhile disciple Mordo, and confronts Mordo about it, only to be prevented from speaking about the threat by a magic spell. He is not prevented from thinking about it, however, and a realization dawns:

> Now at last I see the power of sorcery! I cannot give up! The evil Mordo must *never* be allowed to defeat the Ancient One! For if he should, what would happen to the world as we know it?
>
> (Lee and Ditko 1963: 11)

Without consciously meaning to, Stephen Strange has finally had an unselfish thought and considered others before himself. He now approaches the Ancient One in a much more humble manner and asks to be allowed to study with him and prove himself worthy:

> Ahh! At last I have reached the *real* Dr. Strange! I knew that there was good within you . . . if I could but bring it to the surface! I *accept* you, my son! You shall be my disciple!
>
> (Lee and Ditko 1963: 12)

This is a short and simple story, but the themes it contains are clear and powerful: acting on behalf of others instead of oneself; self-centredness actually leading to the destruction of self; acceptance of the person with flaws (as discussed in Chapter 7), and, finally and most importantly, good overcoming evil, both within the individual and in the wider world.

Compare this to the story of Iron Man, as told in the critically acclaimed 2008 film of the same name. We meet Tony Stark, a very rich, successful playboy who drinks, gambles, womanizes and does not turn up to meetings when expected as he is too busy playing – though he is also something of a natural genius when it comes to weapons design. Stark owes his considerable fortune to Stark Industries, the weapons manufacturing business which was originally set up by his long-deceased father to contribute to the American war effort during the Second World War, and which has been shepherded since his father's death by Obadiah Stane, a close friend of his father and now Stark's business partner.

Stark flies to Afghanistan to unveil his latest weapon to the American forces there (the Jericho missile). During his flight he is criticized for his flippant manner by Colonel Rhodes, the man in charge of his safety:

> You don't respect yourself, so I know you don't respect me. I'm just your babysitter, so when you need your diaper changed let me know, and I'll get you a bottle, okay? You are constitutionally incapable of being responsible.
>
> (Fergus et al. 2008)

Shortly after Stark's arrival in Afghanistan and his presentation of the weapon his escort unit is ambushed and he is captured by a local warlord. His life is saved by a fellow prisoner, Yensin, who is himself being kept alive to be a translator. Stark is appalled to find out that the warlord's forces are also equipped with Stark Industries weaponry. The warlord orders Stark to build a Jericho missile for him. Stark refuses, and is told he has a week to comply or be killed.

> Yensin: Your life's work in the hands of these murderers . . . is this how you want to go out?
> Stark: If I refuse they'll kill me . . . and whatever I do I'll probably be dead in a week.
> Yensin: Then that makes this a very important week for you.
>
> (Fergus et al. 2008)

Stark ostensibly agrees to build the missile, but, with Yensin's aid secretly starts work on a specially powered suit of armour instead. At the very last minute the warlord's forces get suspicious and begin to make their way towards the cave where Stark and Yensin are powering up the armour with Stark inside it. Yensin draws them away with a diversion to buy Stark enough time, but is shot for his trouble. Stark, now wearing the first prototype of what will later become his Iron Man outfit, escapes and overcomes the warlord's forces, but not before he comes across the dying Yensin:

> Stark: Thank you for saving me.
> Yensin: Don't waste it. Don't waste your life.
>
> (Fergus et al. 2008)

As can be seen from these snippets, Yensin's role in the Iron Man story is – like Gandalf's in *Lord of the Rings* – to be the moral conscience that leads the piece. He talks about moral choices in difficult circumstances, and he acts as a moral exemplar through his self-sacrifice on Stark's behalf. Tony Stark now has the moral duty to live up to the chance and opportunity that he has been given, or Yensin's sacrifice would remain wasteful and in vain. This seems to be a theme that can resonate with children as well as adults:

> My dad got me into superheroes, and we watch lots of films together . . . My favourites are Iron Man and Superman . . . I like stories with change, when the characters change. Iron Man becomes a hero. (Year 4 girl)

> He's prisoner and his friend helps him build the first Iron Man suit . . . he dies, and that makes Iron Man more want to save everyone else. (Year 5 boy)

Waste (the theme of Yensin's final moral imperative to Stark) has been traditionally recognized as a type of evil (see Aquinas 2009), whether waste of potential, waste of energy, waste of opportunity, waste of resources, waste of time, or waste of the gifts or talents or chances we are given to do something good or useful. In addition, Rhodes's earlier criticism of Stark (see above) can be seen as one of wastefulness as well as of irresponsibility, as the two things are deeply connected – as Stark begins to see.

Stark now uses his suit to escape from danger, and is rescued by American forces, but the self-sacrifice and the words spoken by Yensin have profoundly affected him. His first major act after returning to America is to call a press conference:

> Stark: I never got to say goodbye to my father. There are questions I would have asked him . . . I would have asked how he felt about what his company did, if he was conflicted, if he ever had doubts . . . I saw young Americans killed by the very weapons I created to defend them and protect them, and I saw that I had become part of a system that has become comfortable with zero accountability.
>
> Journalist: What happened over there?
>
> Stark: I had my eyes opened. I came to realize that I had more to offer this world than just making things to blow up. And this is why, effective immediately, I am shutting down the weapons manufacturing arm of Stark until such a time when I can decide what the future of this company will be, what direction it should take and that I am comfortable with and is compatible with the greatest good for the country as well.
>
> (Fergus et al. 2008)

Tony Stark has had a moral epiphany (or 'changed', as the Year 4 girl put it). He has been forced to think deeply about consequence and purpose for the first time in his life, and while his future life may contain some of its past playboy trappings, it now becomes devoted to causes outside and beyond his own self and circumstances (for example, the 'greatest good'). He has become ready to *deserve* the role of hero (see below) once it arrives later in the story, as the key aspect of superheroes is exactly that they *do* take a moral stand. Stories that are built around superheroes frequently explore steadfastness and self-sacrifice in the service of some idea of the desired 'greater good', something that is not just demonstrated by the Iron Man story. Aquaman, for example, acts in the service of the well-being of the underwater world and its ecology; Catwoman is motivated by her concern for the well-being and good treatment of cats; the X-Men act towards the promotion and achievement of peaceful co-existence between mutants and non-mutants (see Chapter 11); Superman, since the dynamic George Reeves television series of the 1950s, acts in the service of 'truth and justice and the American way' (which is properly understood as not a narrow or partisan patriotism, but rather a shorthand for tolerance, fair treatment under the law, the promotion of democracy and everyone's right to have a voice and be treated as a person), and so on. (We are really back to Aristotle's teleological ethics, only this time it is explored through stories rather than through a logical exploration of reasoned points.)

Being of bad (or evil) character

Tellingly, the two stories discussed above also shed much light on what it is to be a bad or evil character. The Iron Man story has not yet finished; the viewer now finds out that the reason why the warlord's forces were equipped with Stark Industries weaponry is that Obadiah Stane was secretly selling them to him 'under the table', despite the fact that the weapons were to be used against his own countrymen. It appears, in fact, that Obadiah Stane absolutely does not care who gets to benefit from the weapons he sells or what uses they are put to, provided he continues to make a tidy profit from their sale. We also find out that Stane has betrayed Stark; the capture of Stark was no accident – the warlord had been commissioned to capture and kill him so that Stane could regain complete control of the company. Obadiah Stane, it seems, will go to any lengths to achieve his aims, regardless of the consequences or who might get hurt. He is loyal to no one except himself, as we clearly see in a later scene when he visits and confronts the warlord who lets Stark escape and leaves him paralysed. Then as he leaves the scene, he says to his men 'Let's finish off here', which is the chillingly casual cue for them to gun down the entire encampment, killing everyone there in cold blood. Eventually Stane will attack and leave Stark for dead, and it will take the new superhero Iron Man to stop him. Obadiah Stane demonstrates very well that, if a superhero can be understood as someone who puts the 'greater good' before his or her own interest, and seeks to achieve that desired good through morally just actions, then a typical superhero narrative villain can be seen as the exact opposite: someone who puts self-interest and personal gain before all other considerations, including any moral ones – in fact they typically show a disdain for moral issues and believe themselves to be above them. Classical dualism is brought to life through such characters.

The crucial thing, however, is not just that Stane acts in these morally reprehensible ways, but that – just like Mordo in the earlier Dr. Strange story – he pretends to be a good man. His public persona is that of the loyal, trustworthy deputy, but the truth of his moral self is much darker. In other words, he dissembles: he portrays himself as something he is not. He seeks to hoodwink the innocent and the good and take advantage of them, and, if his ambitions would be served by it, is completely happy to destroy them.

This wilful and malicious misrepresentation of self is a common attribute of superhero narrative villains. Superman's nemesis, Lex Luthor, is a great philanthropist and pillar of society publicly – and even President of the United States in many recent Superman narratives (see *Superman/Batman: Public Enemies* (2010) and the last episode of *Smallville* (2011), for example) – but behind his generous and humanitarian façade he is ruthless, extremely dangerous, completely uncaring, entirely self-serving and power-hungry. One of Batman's reappearing villains is Roland Daggett, who, on the face of it, is an upright citizen whose many successful businesses donate to Gotham City's charitable causes, but behind the scenes he is quite willing to pursue unethical and quite ruthless methods to achieve his goals (such as making homeless a whole impoverished community so that his companies can turn a profit building luxury premises on the land they rent their dilapidated apartments on), while always ensuring that his association with anyone who might get caught working on his behalf seems non-existent. Even Loki, the evil brother of Thor, constantly takes pains to appear a loyal, trustworthy and good son to his father Odin.

From these characters and their stories children learn that one aspect of goodness is *transparency*, and, conversely, that one very telling signifier of evil or danger is when the appearance and substance of character *do not match*. This is a very valuable message for children, who are vulnerable to being swayed by how things and people appear (Piaget and Inhelder 1969) and who may not appreciate that danger may lie behind a kindly or friendly face. As Lindon (2008: 200) puts it, 'children are ignorant in the most positive sense of the word; there is so much they do not know' when it comes to the dangers and deceits practised by some members of the world that surrounds them.

Being heroic

Fall of the Blue Beetle!, a *Batman: The Brave and the Bold* animated episode written for younger children (Krieg 2010), combines all the themes explored in this chapter and demonstrates how embedded they are in superhero narratives, and how explicitly children are invited to consider them. The story starts with two young teenagers sharing a meal on a camping trip. Jaime Reyes is telling his friend Paco a story:

> Jaime: The starship plummets through the Earth's atmosphere, pieces of fuselage ripping off before it finally crashes in a remote desert. With the life ebbing from his body, the alien orders his power ring to search the planet for a worthy successor. The ring searches every section of the globe until it finds a man without fear, and a new hero is born!

Paco: Wow, dude, that's amazing. . .ly stupid! That's the best you could come up with for the secret origin of the Green Lantern? [*Though, unknown to Paco and Jaime, it is entirely accurate.*] Gimme a break!

Jaime: What? What's wrong with my story?

Paco: First of all, a dude without fear is a serious mental condition. Secondly, how does a ring choose someone? No, what happened was some ordinary guy just lucked into finding it. Everyone knows it's the ring that's special, not the person wearing it.

(Krieg 2010)

This is a key theme of many superhero narratives; whether it is the powers or the nature of the *person* with the powers that matters. Typically, the villains of any piece desire or admire powers simply because they *are* powers and literally add to their overall store of power, as well as to their chances of achieving their self-interested goals, while what matters to the good characters is the *use* that any powers are put to. This theme is expressed through the many stories that see superheroes go up against foes whose powers duplicate their own, but whose use of them demonstrates a very different moral standpoint, or even the lack of one – for example, *Superman: Doomsday* (2007), which sees Superman battle an amoral doppelganger.

The theme matters deeply to Jaime because, unknown to Paco, he has recently experienced a direct parallel to the Green Lantern origin story. Jaime has recently discovered a strange blue scarab which has turned him into the new Blue Beetle. It is important to Jaime to feel that he was chosen to become the latest Blue Beetle because of something worthwhile in his character, and that his discovery of the scarab was not just a matter of chance:

Jaime: You know what, Paco? You're so wrong! People aren't just handed out powers randomly; there's always a reason! Heroes are chosen because they're worthy to be heroes!

(Krieg 2010)

This, of course, is tapping into a deep and probably unresolvable philosophical question: why some people receive opportunity, power, good fortune, success, strong health, happiness, contentment and so on, while others seem to receive privation, illness, disability, rejection or suffering. In other words, do we merit our situation in life, or does it arise through luck (whether good or ill) or destiny or God's blessing or happenstance; and, perhaps even more troubling, would we rather our situation in life was deserved or arbitrary, as what would either of these possibilities say about us and our existence? Engagement with stories that stimulate thought about this philosophical theme is very useful for children – partly because the theme itself possibly deserves substantial consideration by every person who wishes to consider himself or herself educated, and partly because stories involve characters who are *not* the children themselves – in other words, the theme can be considered at a safe distance.

Jaime suits up as the Blue Beetle and flies off to find his mentor, Batman, to ask him what he thinks. Batman is in the middle of a battle with a minor villain.

> Jaime: Question: Do you think that heroes are chosen, or is it just dumb luck?
> Batman: Blue! Not the best time!
> Jaime: C'mon! This is important! Do you think I was chosen to replace the Blue Beetle because we share the same heroic traits?
> Batman: There've been a lot of Blue Beetles, and you're *nothing* like the one I knew.
>
> (Krieg 2010)

Disheartened, Jaime flies off and carries out his own research into previous Blue Beetles. He discovers the existence of a hidden island, which seems to be the final place that the last Blue Beetle, now revealed to be Ted Kord, was known to go to.

> Jaime: This could be the whole reason I was chosen. Maybe the Beetle's in trouble and I'm the one who's supposed to save him.
>
> (Krieg 2010)

Jaime makes his way to the island where he is met by an impressive, handsome and well-spoken man who introduces himself as his predecessor.

> Kord: So you're my replacement . . . welcome to Science Island. I'm Ted Kord, the Blue Beetle . . . I came to this island to harness the amazing technology of the scarab to benefit all mankind. If humans would just work together we could do anything . . . These are my helpers [*pointing to a whole gallery of scarab-shaped robots*]. They will do the farming to help the poor, the building to house the homeless; just waiting to be powered by the awesome technology of the blue scarab.
> Jaime: About the scarab: why me? Why did I get it?
> Kord: I dream of a perfect world, but I can't do it alone. I sent my scarab in search of an ally. I programmed it to search out someone of good value – someone worthy to inherit the mantle of the Blue Beetle . . . and it found *you*.
>
> (Krieg 2010)

This, of course, is exactly what Jaime wishes to hear, and so he willingly agrees to help. He powers up the entire company of robot scarabs, then leaves. As he does so the child viewer sees Kord smirk nastily. It turns out that Jaime has unwittingly enabled the robot army that Kord intends to take over the world with. Luckily, Batman, who has met Kord before, is on his way to help his young friend, but, even before he arrives, Jaime has realized the truth:

> Jaime: All that stuff about making a better world . . . and I fell for it!
> Kord: Oh no, I'm quite sincere about that. War, conflict, strife; they'll all vanish with humanity under the absolute control of one single leader. Mankind will flourish as I eliminate all –
> Batman: Freedom.
> Kord: It's a small price to pay.
>
> (Krieg 2010)

More will be said about this theme of *freedom* below. In the meantime, Batman and Blue Beetle escape danger and steel up for the final confrontation with Kord. Batman explains (as the child viewer sees these events in flashback):

> Batman: That man *isn't* Ted Kord; it's Jarvis Kord, Ted's uncle. Ted was a brilliant scientist, but he couldn't access the scarab's powers . . . His only mistake was trusting his uncle to unlock the mysteries of the blue scarab . . . Ted made the ultimate sacrifice and in doing so made sure the scarab fell into the right hands – *your* hands, Jaime.
>
> (Krieg 2010)

Batman ensures that Jaime escapes, then faces down Kord as his island explodes, destroying his robot army. Just as it looks like Batman is doomed, the Blue Beetle returns.

> Batman: I told you *not* to wait for me!
> Jaime: Yeah, right!
>
> (Krieg 2010)

The story concludes as they fly to safety in the batplane (the Blue Beetle having rescued Jarvis Kord too):

> Jaime: Look, I'm sorry I got all hung up over the Beetle history lesson. I wanted so badly to have been chosen to be this hero instead of lucking into it. I guess I was an idiot to fall for Kord's story about me being special.
> Batman: The scarab *did* choose. It let *you* access its powers, not Ted. But being chosen doesn't make you a hero; what *you* choose does.

Jaime: I just want to do the right thing . . . like Ted would have done.
Batman [*thinks*]: Spoken like a true hero.

(Krieg 2010)

This story contains all the elements typical to superhero narratives. We see the good characters look after each other and put themselves at risk to save each other, the defeat of a threat to the greater good (in this case freedom), a villain who represents himself as a good man but is anything but, a good character making mistakes but learning from them and having his mistakes accepted by others, and, most tellingly, a message about the importance of individual moral responsibility. Batman's final advice to Jaime, that it is a person's own choices that signify his moral standing (that is, how he plays the cards he has been dealt rather than the cards themselves) is, perhaps, the key feature of superhero narratives (coupled, of course, with the bold reassurance that people are capable of pursuing good moral choices successfully even in the face of evil).

A group of Year 4 and Year 5 children who watched this story were asked the question: 'The Blue Beetle wonders why he received the scarab and became a superhero, doesn't he? So why do you think he did? Was it by luck or because of something else?' One Year 5 boy's response, which drew lots of agreement from the rest of the group was:

Year 5 boy: He got the scarab because he was good and worthy. Like, he came back for Batman and rescued the professor [Jarvis Kord] even though he was the baddie. So he deserved it.
Me: So it wasn't just luck?
Year 5 boy: No.

For this boy, Jaime's status as deserving to be a superhero was justified by his rescuing of Batman and Kord: something that for this class seemed to be the key aspect of superheroes – they save people.

Freedom, rescue, and the triumph of good over evil

All the elements in *Fall of the Blue Beetle!* are deeply attractive and illustrate a strong and definite moral idealism that is one of key appeals of the superhero genre and a core reason why many children find it worth engaging with in the first place. This idealism defines the genre and consists of the idea that good will overcome evil and mankind will progress towards a state of goodness, safety and justice, provided good people enact their goodness and stand up against evil. This is not a new idea, as evidenced by the famous statement attributed to Edmund Burke (1729–1797): 'The only thing necessary for the triumph of evil is for good men to do nothing.'

Superheroes' consistent promotion of this idea can be charted back not just to the superhero comics of the Second World War, when Batman, Robin, Wonder Woman, Superman, Captain America, the Boy Commandos and many more stood up against Hitler and his Nazis, but to the first real superhero of all, Baroness Orczy's *The Scarlet Pimpernel* (1905/2007). A quick look at this character demonstrates this very well.

The date is 1792, the time of the French Revolution, and Sir Percy Blakeney lives in aristocratic comfort in his English home, along with his wife, the beautiful Marguerite. She, along with virtually everyone who has dealings with Sir Percy, regards him as a fop and a disappointment, a spoilt rich man who fritters his life away on frivolous pursuits and is quite useless both domestically and in the wider world – which is very similar to the way the socialite Bruce Wayne is often perceived by others with real jobs in Gotham City. Marguerite frets about the state of the world, while Sir Percy plays cards and only seems to worry about whether his appearance is fashionable or not.

Unbeknown to all, however, Sir Percy dons the mask and costume of the 'Scarlet Pimpernel' and, aided by his gang of like-minded fellows, enters France illegally, rescues people from the guillotine and brings them to England where they can be safe. No one knows his secret identity. Soon the Scarlet Pimpernel has built up a reputation for success, bravery and derring-do, and Marguerite berates her hapless husband for not being enough like him – just as Lois Lane perpetually complains to Clark Kent that he should be more like Superman.

The Scarlet Pimpernel's growing reputation, however, soon means that an arch-enemy emerges in the form of Chauvelin, the chief French spy-catcher, who, for Orczy, personalizes all the tyranny, brutality and injustice meted out by Robespierre, Danton and others responsible for the acts of the French Revolution, and the later books in the series often focus on the duel of wits between the two men as a shorthand for the duel between Good and Evil. This personification of classical dualism is made quite explicit by Orczy, but, as with all good superhero stories subsequently written, often with wry humour, as the blurb for Orczy's *The Laughing Cavalier* (first published in 1914) shows:

> The year is 1623, the place Haarlem in the Netherlands. Diogenes – the first Sir Percy Blakeney the Scarlet Pimpernel's ancestor – and his friends Pythagoras and Socrates defend justice . . . The famous artist Frans Hals also makes an appearance in this historical adventure: Orczy maintains that Hal's celebrated portrait *The Laughing Cavalier* is actually a portrayal of the Scarlet Pimpernel's ancestor.
>
> (Orczy 1914/2011: back cover)

The choice of names – Diogenes, Pythagoras and Socrates – clearly demonstrates Orczy's reverence for the moral teaching of the Ancient Greeks, and shows that her hero, Sir Percy Blakeney, is to be understood not just as a man of action but as a moral exemplar and an agent of Good. Good and Sir Percy, needless to say, always win – though not always easily and not always without sacrifice.

The important thing is that Sir Percy refuses to do nothing in the face of tyranny and evil, but acts on his moral principles to defeat them, despite the risk and danger to himself. This is what all superheroes do: they serve as role models of positive and able moral agents who have a profound sense of moral responsibility and act on it – as can be seen in Ben Grimm's final words to Reed Richards once the group have discovered their new superpowers in the very first *Fantastic Four* story ever written:

> Ben Grimm: You don't have to make a speech, big shot! We've gotta *use* that power to help mankind, right?
> Reed Richards: Right, Ben, right!
>
> (Lee and Kirby 1961: 32)

It is also telling that the themes explored in stories featuring all super-heroes from the Scarlet Pimpernel onwards, namely freedom, rescue, the thwarting of the villain and the restoration of the good, are also the common themes of children's superhero play, as illustrated in this mother's recollection:

> One of [. . .]'s earliest superhero games, when he was between 2 and 3, was when he would rescue me. I had to go to a radiator in the kitchen and say 'Help, I'm trapped!' or something like that. Then [. . .] would say 'Don't worry, Mummy, I'm coming', and he would come and release me from the radiator, saying, 'There you are, Mummy, you're safe now', and put his arms around me. We played this again and again. Later on, as he grew older, the game changed a little. We've got two sofas in the sitting room, and [. . .] and I would sit on one of them, while [. . .]'s daddy had to be the baddy and take [. . .]'s special teddy-bear and hide it under a cushion on the other sofa. [. . .] would then defeat his daddy with his superpowers in some way and rescue his teddy and bring it back to our sofa, then Daddy would have to creep up and capture it again, and the whole game would begin again.

The chase games that form much of superhero play (see Holland 2003), as well as involving the heroes and villains perpetually running and leaping after each other, also often develop to involve a third party – a person or group of people that get captured and need rescuing. While the games themselves are really composed of physical delight and exuberance (see Chapter 5), they tap into the deep moral themes of freedom, rescue and desired good that have been explored during this chapter. The following chapters will explore how specific superheroes manifest these themes and suggest some learning ideas to pursue them.

PART III
Exploring superhero narratives

9   Superman: the god-like being

The character of Superman provides an opportunity for children to explore ideas about God, the nature and source of goodness and the just use of power.

Introduction

> Jimmy Olsen: Gosh, Miss Lane, I think he really cares for you.
> Lois Lane: Oh . . . Superman cares for everybody, Jimmy.
> *Superman the Movie* (Puzo et al. 1978)

Superman is perhaps the most iconic and important superhero there is. Every single superhero who has followed in his wake has either modelled himself or herself on his template or actively rejected it, but, either way, Superman remains the key frame of reference for defining what a superhero is. Similarly, the approach to moral issues exemplified by Superman and explored in his stories sets the tone for all other superhero narratives, as will be seen.

Superman arrived on Earth in June 1938, courtesy of two Jewish teenagers who lived in Cleveland, USA, Jerome Siegel and Joe Shuster. This was the time of the Great Depression, the rise of fascism in Europe and of Stalin in the USSR, and the slide towards war with Nazi Germany and the other Axis powers. The publication of *Action Comics #1* became a landmark event in the culture of the time, introducing a new, dynamic figure who was strong – not strong in the cruel and brutal way that Hitler and Stalin were strong, but strong and *just*. His powers (which were to increase considerably over the years that followed) were immediately put to the service of those who were oppressed or in danger or in dire need.

The champion of justice

A good example of this can be found in the very first issue of Superman's own comic, *Superman #1* (1939), where the theme of *justice* springs out from almost every page:

> Clark decided he must turn his titanic strength into channels that would benefit mankind. And so was created – SUPERMAN champion of the oppressed, the physical marvel who had sworn to devote his existence to helping those in need!
>
> (Siegel and Shuster 1939: 4)

The several stories that follow are indicative of this stance, as a quick glance at their subject matter confirms:

- Superman scatters a lynch mob and reverses a miscarriage of justice, saving an innocent man from execution by unmasking the real murderess.
- Superman takes on a crooked politician whose unlawful dealings with a munitions magnate threaten to draw the country into war so the two of them can make a profit.
- Superman confronts a mine owner who knowingly puts his workers in unsafe conditions to maximize his profit margins.
- Superman opposes a corrupt coach who hires professional thugs to nobble players on the opposing team.
- Superman prevents a habitual domestic abuser meting out violence to women.

It is worth observing that the evils Superman opposes at the very beginning of his career are very human, very troubling and very *real*. At this stage in his career Superman protects the innocent not from death rays from the stars or being swallowed by another dimension or other such imaginary and unlikely fates, but from very familiar and actual evils that humans visit upon each other, things that actually happen to real people. Even later, when Superman's villains become more fantastical and unrealistic (such as Braniac and Darkseid), he still consistently confronts real causes of harm and suffering. In his time Superman has helped raise money for hospital rebuilding, worked against adult and child illiteracy, stood up against the use of landmines, fought racial discrimination, promoted and argued for the proper treatment of animals, attempted to destroy the entire human stock of nuclear weapons, and attempted to eradicate hunger, among other things (Khan 2006). Other superheroes have engaged in such real-life causes, but Superman was the first to do so and the others follow in his wake. Superman, in fact, has a long history of standing up for people who are in situations that make them powerless to stand up for themselves – as is made explicit in 12-year-old Tommy Delaney's letter to Superman in *Superman for the Animals* (2000) – a free Superman comic sponsored by the Doris Day Animal Foundation:

> You inspired me to do the right thing . . . and you did it just by being who you are. I realized I don't need to be Superman to stand up for what's right! You showed me that being a hero isn't about being tough or throwing your weight around. It's really about being willing to help those who can't fight for themselves.
>
> (Millar 2000: 17)

It is perhaps not altogether surprising that Superman emerged into the world at such a miserable time in human history and was a product of two Jewish creators in a period of great and explicit anti-Semitism. Many felt helpless against the massive forces of the depression and Nazism and totalitarianism the world over. Siegel recalled: 'I am lying in bed counting sheep when all of a sudden it hits me. I conceive a character like Samson, Hercules, and all the strong men I have ever heard of rolled into one. Only more so' (quoted in Fingeroth 2004: 13). Superman served (and still serves) as a bold figure of wish-fulfilment; a character who *could* stand up against such massive forces of oppression and hardship, 'the greatest exponent of justice the world has ever known' (Siegel and Shuster 1939: 7), a character who was just as well as strong.

Importantly (as will be shown below), even though he is a man of great power and deals with large-scale issues like those listed above, no cause or source of unhappiness or sorrow is too small for Superman to concern himself with. It is only partly tongue-in-cheek that Superman rescues a cat from a tree and returns it to the upset child in *Superman the Movie* (Puzo et al. 1978); the scene is meant to indicate that Superman has time for all causes of distress, even little ones; he is not above helping those who worry or suffer because of them. Superman *does* care for everyone, as Lois rightly observes, and it is this above all that marks him out as special.

In addition, and seen from his very first stories, Superman's response to the crime or unethical behaviour at hand is always *proportional* to that behaviour; in other words, his response matches the offence. (Being able to determine proportionality was a most important aspect of moral reasoning, according to Kohlberg (1984), as this demonstrated that children were able to recognize a key signifier of fairness and fair treatment.) All the stories in *Superman #1* contain a considerable amount of fair and, indeed, poetic justice: the munitions magnate is taken to the front line to see what it feels like to be at the receiving end of the weapons he manufactures, the mine owner is taken into his unsafe mine to see what it is like to be frightened by the possibility of suffocation or mine shafts collapsing, the man who threatens women gets to feel what it is like to fear the retribution of someone more powerful than he is, and so on. Superman, it seems, brings justice through using his superpowers not only to prevent poor, unjust or harmful consequences from unfolding, but also to put the perpetrators of injustice in their victims' shoes so that they become less blasé about their behaviour and *change their ways*. This theme – which is really the theme of reformation of character – remains a constant as the number of Superman stories produced grows over the decades.

A certain requirement arises here: if Superman was to have the moral authority as well as the physical power to be able to confront people with their own moral failings, then it follows that he needed to be an exemplary moral role model himself. He also needed to be in a position which would allow him to be a moral observer of mankind. It was, perhaps, the realization of this dual requirement that would lead to the evolution of the character in a very interesting and significant way.

The innately good character in a tarnished world

Superman's arrival from the planet Krypton initially served the function of providing the explanation for the existence of his superpowers, but it did not take long before more was made of it. First of all, Superman is a 'strange visitor from another planet' (Maxwell and Luber 1951/2005); the important thing being that he is *not human*. This absolves him of any responsibility for the situation the human beings around him find themselves in through their poor or immoral or selfish historical choices: Superman is not part of the species that seems perpetually prone to violence, oppression or hatred; he does not share our flawed human nature or the shameful episodes of our human history – our inherited guilt, if you will.

This allows him to look at human behaviour as an outside observer, which in turn enables him to have two further roles in his stories: to act as a moral commentator on the strengths and failings of human behaviour; and to prevent the poor consequences of unethical human behaviour from happening and put things right again. The spectacle of Superman's dramatic and physical response to acts of foolishness, selfishness, recklessness or malice is often accompanied by his thoughts about those who have committed these acts: thoughts, it is worth noting, which tend to be generous-minded and sympathetic more often than not.

Secondly, Superman's arrival on Earth as a baby necessitated his being raised by Jonathan and Martha Kent on their farm in Smallville, Kansas. Having established Superman's nature as a Kryptonian, the narratives surrounding him went on to establish his very *human* nurture. He is brought up by good, unprivileged folk working the land, and learns traditionally good values: honesty, loyalty, the importance of earning one's keep, humility, restraint, moderation, consideration, courtesy, respect for others, a forgiving nature, and so on – indeed, young Clark Kent is raised to have and to value all the traditional virtues as identified by Aristotle (2004) and Aquinas (2009). A great many stories show Ma and Pa Kent involved in the moral education of their son, primarily by example but often explicitly through words (including, for the benefit of the reader, thought bubbles that make clear Ma or Pa Kent's responses to Clark's moral choices and behaviour), and the adult Clark that they produce is always portrayed as someone who wishes to find the best in everyone.

Clark's moral values make him stand out when he finally leaves home and enters the big city. His small-town upbringing and rather naïve and innocent world-view (in the eyes of his *Daily Planet* colleagues) are often contrasted with the shadier and more sordid realities which are part and parcel of Metropolis and its often more jaded approaches to life. (A lovely example of this can be found in *Superman the Movie* (Puzo et al. 1978). It is Clark's first day at the *Daily Planet* and Lois overhears him arranging to have a percentage of his salary paid into a certain account each month. 'Your bookie, right?' she says, before continuing, 'No, don't tell me, your little old grey-haired mother!' Clark replies, 'Umm, silver-haired, actually', wrong-footing her completely.) Whether in his Clark Kent or Superman identities, Superman exemplifies moral values and an ethical approach to life that have been regarded highly since the time of Aristotle and even the Ten Commandments.

The emphasis on the importance of nurture and upbringing in producing a person's moral character is explored as an ongoing theme in the television series *Smallville* (2001–2011), set when Clark is still growing up and has yet to adopt the persona of Superman. One of Clark's neighbours and – to begin with – friends in Smallville is Lex Luthor, who is a few years older than him. The series introduces a new character to the Superman mythos, Lex's father Lionel Luthor, and great play is made of the contrast between the upbringing of the two boys. Clark is brought up in the manner described above, while Lex is brought up by a ruthless man who is steeped in shady business and scientific ethics, and who puts power and wealth before any other considerations. The Kents and the Luthors operate on quite different ethical norms. The question offered is to what extent Lex's and Clark's different upbringings are responsible for their eventual evolution into one of the world's best men and the one of the world's most evil.

Two reasons, therefore, are given for Superman's exemplary goodness of character: his *nature* (he is biologically a Kryptonian – and, as we perpetually hear, Kryptonians are far more evolved and advanced than humans), and his *nurture* (he is brought up well by Jonathan and Martha Kent – and even Jor-El, his natural father, is commonly portrayed as a good man and a kind of hero, attempting, as he does, to save all his fellow Kryptonians from the doom he knows awaits their planet). It is the combination of the two that produces Superman, just as it produces real people too (see Coles 1997). Clark seems naturally predisposed to good, but in the comics and in the television series *Lois and Clark: The New Adventures of Superman* (1993–1996) and the first five series of *Smallville* (2001–2006), he frequently asks for his parents' moral guidance and reassurance. This humanizes him and adds to his usefulness as a good moral role model for children: he is not good in a way that is unattainable, nor is he good in a way that is effortless or without the possibility of making errors. Just like the children who might engage with him (see Piaget 1932/1965; Kohlberg 1984), Superman's goodness is, to a great extent, established through the education, support and acceptance offered by the people who bring him up; and it is rather reassuring to see the greatest and most powerful hero of all time on the telephone to his mother and father for advice.

This theme – what causes characters to be good or evil, whether this is to do with some inherent trait of the person, or a product of circumstances, upbringing or even destiny – is a powerful and regular component of many superhero narratives. An episode of the second series of *Smallville* (2002) explores this theme in a most interesting manner. At this moment in the story, Clark Kent has just learned that he is not human after all, but instead landed on Earth in a spaceship while a baby. Jonathan and Martha Kent have kept the tiny vehicle hidden in their storm-cellar (it is Kansas, after all), and now Clark decides to do what a great number of real-life adopted children do, even if they love their foster-parents very much and wholeheartedly regard them as their parents (see Eldridge 1999): he seeks to find out about his biological parents in case the knowledge he gains sheds some light on his identity. As a result, he decides to look inside the spaceship for the first time, with Jonathan Kent being a supportive father at his side.

As they open the spaceship, Kryptonian writing appears. Jonathan, of course, cannot read it, but it looks as if Clark can. What he reads troubles him immensely:

Jonathan: What is it, son?
Clark: It's a message from my biological father . . . I'm sure I'm reading it wrong.
Jonathan: Why? What does it say?
Clark: 'On this third planet from the star, Sol, you be god among men. They are a flawed race; rule them with strength, my son. That is where your greatness lies.'
[*Upset*] I think I was sent here to conquer! What kind of a planet am I from?
Jonathan: Maybe you did misread it, Clark, but even if you didn't, it's *you* who decides what kind of a life you're going to lead. *You*. Not me, not your mother, not your . . . biological parents.

Clark: What if it's part of who I am?

Jonathan: [*Putting his arms around Clark*] Clark Kent, you're here to be a force for Good, not for Evil.

Clark: But how can you be so sure?

Jonathan: Because *I* am your father. *I* raised you . . . and I know you better than anyone.

(Gough and Millar 2002)

This scene closes the episode and opens up many of the traditional and philosophical questions about identity and character that have ever existed. Is one's identity and type of life pre-ordained (whether genetically, attitudinally, behaviourally, morally or otherwise)? Are we products of our upbringing, with the apple not falling too far from the tree? Is identity fixed or changing? Or do we exercise free will over who we are and who we become? Jonathan Kent offers his son two assurances at once: it is up to Clark who he becomes (so, free will), but also that he, Jonathan, raised Clark in such a way that he is destined to be a good man (so, nurture and upbringing). The viewer is invited to ask: could Clark Kent grow up to become an evil person, perhaps using his superpowers for ill, or could he even grow up to reject his powers entirely and not use them for good or evil? Engagement with this story could provide a very rich vein to mine in children's Philosophy lessons (see below), or even in university courses that explore child development theory for student teachers and early years professionals.

The friend

As well as being of good character, Superman, like Aristotle, has an overriding concern with the establishment of the 'desired good' (see Chapter 8); something that has been long recognized. Consider this extract from Galloway (1973), for example:

> There is a not-so-subtle aspect to the job description of our beloved Kryptonian. It is not mentioned as publicly as, say, his fight for justice . . . Superman seems, in fact, to have another primary reason for being: the health, wealth and happiness of . . . persons.
>
> (Galloway 1973: 75)

This comes over strongly when Clark makes his first public appearance as Superman in the *Superman the Movie* (1978) – a film that has become canonical in the Superman mythos (see Skelton 2006). In this scene, which has had homages paid to it in the film *Superman Returns* (2006) and the last series of *Smallville* (2011), Lois Lane boards a helicopter on the helipad on top of the

Daily Planet building. The vehicle goes out of control, however, and crashes on the very edge of the roof. It is obvious that it will soon plummet down to the street some distance below. Lois attempts to climb out to safety, but falls, only to be scooped up in mid-air by a strange figure in a red, yellow and blue costume.

> Superman: Easy, Miss; I've got you.
> Lois: You've got me?! Who's got you?
>
> (Puzo et al. 1978)

After catching the helicopter (which did fall), returning it and Lois to safety on the roof, and organizing help for the injured pilot, Superman faces Lois.

> Superman: Well, I certainly hope this little episode hasn't put you off flying, Miss. Statistically speaking, it's still the safest way to travel.
>
> (Puzo et al. 1978)

He then makes to leave, but Lois stops him.

> Lois: Stop! Who *are* you?
> Superman [*smiles*]: A friend.
>
> (Puzo et al. 1978)

This is more significant than it may seem. Superman could have said anything to introduce himself and explain his presence; that he was a Kryptonian, that he was Superman, even that he was a champion of justice; but he chose to introduce himself as a *friend*. A friend is someone who helps you, understands you and supports you, someone who is sympathetic to you and who listens to you. This is not the way, for instance, that Batman would normally introduce himself (see Chapter 10), and it serves to show that Superman, even though he is not human, is on humanity's side. A friend cares for you and looks after you, which is exactly what Superman does.

This becomes even more important when another reading of Superman is taken into consideration, as will now be explained.

The metaphor for God

Superheroes are often understood as heroic figures in the Judeo-Christian tradition (such as Samson) as each one, to a great extent, is a synthesis of

> elements of the selfless hero who gives his life for others and the zealous crusader who destroys evil. The supersaviors in pop culture

function as replacements for the Christ figure . . . their superhuman abilities reflect a hope for divine, redemptive powers.

(Jewett and Lawrence 2002: 6)

This is particularly true in the case of Superman, whose parallels to Christ go one step further. The combination of Superman's other-worldliness, his almost limitless power, his deep goodness and his care for humanity – along with features of his origin story – has led to a quite persuasive understanding of the figure as a Messianic character (it is no accident that the theme tune for the television series *Smallville* is 'Save Me' by Remy Zero) and a metaphor for ideas about God, particularly Jesus Christ. This idea found expression as early as 1973 in Galloway's *The Gospel According to Superman*, which compared Clark's humble demeanour and Superman's acts of rescue and championing of justice to equivalent aspects of character and mission shown by Jesus. There are many other parallels, however. Both Christ and Superman: had parentage which was not human; came to Earth as children; began their work as adults; had powers beyond those of mortal man; lived among humans as humans; and came to Earth to save mankind from the consequences of its sinful behaviour.

The last of these points plays out differently for Jesus and Superman (as you would expect): Jesus saves mankind from the consequences of its sinful behaviour through the salvation of the soul and the overcoming of death, while Superman saves mankind from the consequences of its sinful behaviour through, for instance, stopping the bullet hitting its intended victim and causing death in the first place. In *Superman the Movie* (1978), however, Superman *does* reverse death: Lois dies in the final chapter of the film and a grief-stricken Superman holds her dead body in his hands before turning back time so he can get to Lois before she is killed in a landslide. Returning someone from death, it must be suggested, makes all other superpowers redundant, and cements Superman's status as a saviour and a god-like figure.

Other elements of *Superman the Movie* (1978) contribute to the reading of Superman as a Christ figure too. Consider the words of Jor-El that baby Kal-El absorbs as he travels in the spaceship that is bringing him to Earth:

> Live as one of them, Kal-El, but always hold in your heart the pride of your special heritage. They can be a great people, Kal-El – they wish to be. They only lack the light to show the way. For this reason above all, their capacity for Good, I have sent them you – my only son.
>
> (Puzo et al. 1978)

This, as Skelton (2006) observes, draws on the Gospel of St. John, with echoes of 'I have come into the world as a light' (John 12: 46) and 'For God so loved the world that he gave his one and only Son' (John 3: 16), and it reads like an imagined message from God to Jesus. Christopher Reeve, the actor who played Superman in this film (and also a non-Christian), recalled:

> During the Superman years I received hundreds of letters explaining that Jor-el is God and his son Kal-el (Superman) is Christ, sent from Krypton to be raised by a humble family in Kansas before beginning his mission to save the world. I could appreciate the obvious parallel, and I did consider Superman to be a significant mythical icon.
>
> (Reeve 2003: 141)

Christopher Reeve was not the only person involved in the creation of Superman stories to be aware of this dimension of the character. Mark Millar, a writer of Superman (for example, *Superman for the Animals*, 2000) stated: 'Growing up, I had three moral guides: my family, Jesus, and Superman. The first Christopher Reeve movie was the Third Testament as far as I was concerned' (quoted in Skelton 2006: 1).

The final parallel between Jesus and Superman that is worth noting is that, like Jesus, Superman dies and returns from the dead. In the animated feature *Superman: Doomsday* (2007) and comic-book series *The Death of Superman* (Jurgens 1993) that it was based on, Superman finally meets his match in the form of Doomsday, a monstrous 'intergalactic serial killer' (Capizzi and Timm 2007). As he staggers from their final encounter into Lois's arms he asks weakly:

Superman: Is everyone—?
Lois: You did it, Superman. We're safe. All of us.
Superman: Good. That's . . . that's all that matters. [*Dies*]
(Capizzi and Timm 2007)

The dead Superman is buried under a huge stone (shaped like his famous 'S' shield), but just at the moment that the world realizes that it needs him, he returns from the dead to serve mankind once more.

It is reasonable to suggest that none of these parallels (being sent to Earth by Jor-El, saving people from death, returning from death himself, and so on) would have resonated in the way that they seem to have done without Superman's consistent goodness and the establishment of his mission to do good to the world and care for it. It is Superman's status as an exemplary role model of good character combined with the moral choices he makes about how to use his power that makes all the difference and defines the character. Brandon Routh, who played the character in the film *Superman Returns* (2006) stated:

> Superman is and always will be who he is because of what he symbolises. What he stands for is bigger than that artist who draws

him or the actor who portrays him. Yet the 'S' [on his chest] is always present, as are Truth, Justice, Love and Compassion for those who inhabit this Earth.

(Routh 2006: 115)

It is significant that the whole approach of all *Superman* narratives is optimistic and positive (unlike Batman ones, for instance – see Chapter 10). Like his father Jor-El, Superman regards humanity as having 'the capacity for good', and, as we saw in Chapter 2, Superman himself believes that 'Man is basically *good!* He may do bad things at times . . . but, in the end, his good nature must triumph!' (Haney et al. 1974: 1). So, Superman believes in *us* – in fact, just like Jesus, it seems he 'did not come to judge the world, but to save it' (John 12:47). He is, as discussed above, a 'friend'. Most believers in God wish and believe Him to care about their individual lives, feelings and situations and not be so all-powerful and distant that our little lives make no difference to Him (see Ward 2002). Superman is cast squarely in this mould. He does care for everyone. This seems to be recognized by children as well as adults:

> I like Superman. He's so helpful – and he's a person you'd like to be saved by.

(Year 4 girl)

Learning ideas

Because Superman is both a hugely powerful superhero and an exemplary role model of good character, he offers great possibilities for children to explore and consider ideas about the proper exercise of power and the nature of any good outcome that might be desired. This leads to teaching opportunities that are very much related to Personal, Social and Health Education (PSHE), Citizenship and Ethics in the first instance, with further potential for use of the character in RE and Philosophy. This section offers a list of suggested learning prompts.

The Superman Charter

This is a version of children determining the behavioural expectations of their class. Children could be asked to identify what types of behaviour would be likely to find favour (and disfavour) with Superman, and explain why. The class could then earn their place as official helpers of Superman by exhibiting the good behaviour they have identified over a period of time.

The perfect world

Superman came from the planet Krypton, which was much more advanced that Earth. Children could be invited to identify ways in which it was more advanced. They could then think of ways that they would like Earth to develop so it could become more advanced too. This could include long-term ambitions and initial steps that might lead in the right direction. Finally, children could be asked what would make the world perfect, and why.

What would Superman do?

The free comic *Superman for the Animals* (2000) included a competition which invited readers to tell Superman and DC Comics how they would help animals if they had Superman's powers. This idea could be applied to virtually any issue that children engage with in Citizenship or Ethics; for example, how they would eradicate hunger or inequality or prejudice.

What would Superman do? (2)

Children could be presented with scenarios involving perpetrators of poor behaviour such as employers who do not treat their employees well, people who are habitually violent or lose their temper, people who are dishonest, and so on. They could then be asked to determine a response by Superman that would involve a mixture of the use of power and the use of reasoned argument; in other words, they could be asked to decide how Superman might convince people to change their behaviour. The scenarios presented to children could be made up to suit the educational theme at hand, or could be in actual Superman comics (such as *Superman #1*).

What should Superman not do?

Older children could watch an extract from the animated feature *Superman: Doomsday* (2007), which involves a doppelganger of Superman using his equivalent powers for what he believes is the greater good, but without any of Superman's moral restraint. Is the super-doppelganger right in killing the Toymaster in response to his murder of a child because other children will now be safer? This could be the stimulus for discussion about proportional response and moral principles. Children could discuss what limitations should be applied when determining how to respond to crime or other forms of poor behaviour. This could lead into an exploration of issues such as the principles that might lie behind any state justice system and specifics such as the moral rights and wrongs of, for example, having a death penalty.

What should Superman not do? (2)

Another version of this would be to get children to watch an extract from the film *Superman: The Quest for Peace* (1987) in which Superman resolves to destroy the entire stock of nuclear weapons. Is this a proper use of his powers or is it an interference in human self-determination? In other words, should people decide for themselves what their world is like or have this dictated to them by someone more powerful? With older children this could lead to an exploration of historical uses of power, and even (in RE) the question of whether God should intervene in human affairs or not.

The message to a child

Jor-El and Lara send baby Kal-El off to Earth in a spaceship. In most retellings of the story since the 1970s Kal-El is also equipped with messages from his biological parents – messages that advise him about his role, purpose and character. Children could be asked to put themselves in Jor-El's and Lara's shoes and write a message for baby Kal-El. They could then consider what messages they would give to their own non-superpowered children should they have them in the future.

Humility

Why does Superman not always appear as Superman? Why does he spend time presenting himself to the world as Clark Kent, a much less powerful and more awkward person? Using carefully chosen clips from *Superman the Movie* (1978) or *Lois and Clark: The New Adventures of Superman* (1993–1996), children could explore the possible merits of not being a braggart or show-off, but of quietly getting on with doing good things.

Free will and destiny

Older children (and, indeed, adults) could explore why Clark Kent becomes Superman. To what extent is this because of his Kyptonian heritage (which includes, importantly, his biological capacity to have superpowers in the first place), his upbringing on Earth or his freedom of choice? Students could explore ideas about identity formation, destiny and opportunity. This theme could be developed as deeply as one liked, and end up referring to philosophical and theological ideas throughout the ages.

Does the world deserve a Superman?

In the film *Superman Returns* (2006) we hear about a newspaper article that Lois had previously written, entitled 'Why the World Doesn't Need Superman'.

Later in the film we see her begin a new article called 'Why the World Needs Superman'. Children could be split into two groups to determine (and possibly write) the content of both these articles, then present them to each other before deciding which group put forward the stronger argument. This would help develop children's capacity to mount a case – something that will be increasingly useful as they progress through education.

Alternatively, or as a follow-up, children could do a version of the same activity, but this time the articles would be titled 'Why the World Deserves Superman' and 'Why the World Does Not Deserve Superman'. This would give children a vehicle for exploring ideas about the nature of humanity and to what extent we are good creatures or not. For older children this could easily move into a discussion or exploration of whether humanity deserves God or not.

The list of learning opportunities involving Superman (and, indeed, all superheroes) is probably endless, but this serves to give a flavour of the type of potential that exists. Other superheroes offer other learning possibilities as well as versions of some of the ones suggested above, as will be seen in the following chapters.

10 Batman: darkness within the Dark Knight

Batman provides an opportunity for children to explore ideas about attachment and loss, human suffering, immorality, amorality and evil.

Introduction

> Batman: Starting today, we fight *ideas* with *better ideas*. The idea of *crime* with the idea of *Batman*. From *today* on, Batman will be everywhere it's *dark*, no place to *hide*.
>
> Batman: The Return (Morrison 2012: 18)

Superman narratives might be universally optimistic and positive, but many narratives about Batman tend to be much darker in tone. In fact, there seem to be two Batmen that emerge since the character's first appearance in Kane and Finger's *The Case of the Chemical Syndicate* in 1939: a dark, grim avenger of wrongdoing who persecutes criminals single-mindedly, full of an all-consuming revulsion against crime (especially crime against the person) and a need to ensure that people are spared the suffering that comes from becoming victims of crime; and a more child-friendly KA-*POW!*-type square-jawed, clean-cut Batman (such as that played by Adam West in the 1960s) who climbs walls with his batrope and acts as a mentor (and sometimes guardian) to the young and inexperienced and as a protector of the innocent. Both of these Batmen overlap at times, and both exhibit other distinctive features of the character too. Unlike Superman, he is not blessed with any superpowers but utilizes a whole range of remarkable gadgets and vehicles in their place. He is fit and athletic, a brilliant detective, and a man with a clear mission and purpose. He has his moments of humour – though this is often a very dry or ironic humour – but also his moments of doubt, which are deeply played upon by the villains who inhabit his world.

Whichever of these two Batmen seems most at hand, however, the character remains dark, his very reason for being emanating from the murder of his parents when he was a boy. In the Batman narratives designed especially with children in mind, this circumstance is presented very carefully (for example, in both the animated *Batman: The Brave and the Bold* episode *Invasion of the Secret Santas!* (Beechen 2009) and the current *Batman Live World Arena Tour* (Berkowitz et al. 2011–), the murder of Bruce Wayne's parents is presented off-screen, with only two bullet-shot sounds, two flashes of light and young Bruce's voice crying 'Mother! Father!' signifying what has happened) but the reader or viewer is never allowed to forget that this event is what lies behind the emergence of the character. Similarly, the landscape for Batman narratives is equally dark, both in terms of setting and drawing or cinematic style. Superman's home of Metropolis seems to represent the shiny, cultural and industrious side of a city's life when compared to Batman's home of Gotham City, which equally represents its seedy and dirty underbelly. With regard to visual style, Feiffer observed as long ago as 1965 that 'Batman inhabited a world where no one, no matter the time of day, cast anything but long shadows – seen from weird perspectives. Batman's world was scary; Superman's, never' (Feiffer 1965: 27–28).

In England at the time of writing Batman probably has more exposure than Superman, with two different Batman comics appearing monthly on supermarket shelves, the animated television series *Batman: The Brave and the Bold* and the just-released Batman film *The Dark Knight Rises* (Nolan 2012) starring Christian Bale, advertisements for which are everywhere. In other words, children (and adults) *know* about Batman, so the character has much potential to be used to engage them with some very deep issues about morality and, indeed, amorality, immorality, and questions about human suffering. If Superman narratives explore what the nature of goodness might be, then Batman ones explore the nature of evil and suffering and why they should be resisted, as will now be seen.

Batman, attachment, loss and grief

The origin story of Batman is well known, and a marked contrast to the mythical-scale origin story of Superman. Dr. Thomas Wayne and his wife Martha are returning from taking their young son Bruce to see a film at the cinema (later revealed to be *The Mask of Zorro*, a reference by Bob Kane to one of his inspirations for the character of Batman) when a gunman seizes Martha Wayne's pearls. Thomas Wayne attempts to prevent the theft, resulting in the criminal shooting the two of them, then running off and leaving Bruce Wayne with his dying parents. The famous scene from *Batman #1* (1940) goes like this:

Narrator: The boy's eyes are wide with terror and shock as the horrible scene is spread before him.

Bruce Wayne: Father . . . Mother! . . . Dead! They're d . . . dead.

Narrator: Days later, a curious and strange scene takes place.

Bruce Wayne: [*Praying to God*] And I swear by the spirits of my parents to avenge their deaths by spending the rest of my life warring on all criminals.

Narrator: As the years pass Bruce Wayne prepares himself for his career. He becomes a master scientist. Trains his body to physical perfection until he is able to perform amazing athletic feats.

Bruce Wayne: Dad's estate left me wealthy. I am ready . . . but first I must have a disguise. Criminals are a superstitious cowardly lot, so my disguise must be able to strike terror into their hearts. I must be a creature of the night, black, terrible . . . a . . .

Narrator: As if in answer, a huge bat flies in the open window!

Bruce Wayne: A bat! That's it! It's an omen . . . I shall become a *bat*!

Narrator: And thus is born this weird figure of the dark . . . this avenger of evil, the *BATMAN*.

(Kane 1940: 2)

The creature Batman is born out of human suffering, and can be best understood as Bruce Wayne's sustained response to his grief and premature bereavement of his good and loving parents – an extreme version of separation protest, if you like. Years before John Bowlby's *Child Care and the Growth of Love* (1953/1965), the story of Batman explores in a fantastical way what happens to a child when he loses his parents, and it seems that this story shares some of Bowlby's and other later writers' perspectives. According to Bowlby (1979/2000: 15):

> Like adults, infants and children who have lost a loved one experience grief and go through periods of mourning . . . [These] coincide with and mask strong residual yearning for, and anger with, the lost person . . . the mourning processes of childhood habitually take a course that in older children and adults is regarded as pathological.

For Bruce Wayne the mourning process leads to his becoming fixated on fulfilling his vow to his dead parents, to what seems to be the detriment of his ability to form many normal types of human relationship; for example, any deep romantic relationship with a woman, despite being surrounded by them in his persona as a millionaire playboy. However, there is a core to what he does that speaks more to the notion of 'strong residual yearning' (Bowlby 1979/2000: 50) for his parents than it does to any notion of pathological response. This is expressed by Murray Parkes (1998: 6) in his discussion of bereavement:

'The pain of grief is just as much a part of life as the joy of love; it is, perhaps, the price we pay for love, the cost of commitment.'

For this author, at least, a proper reading of Batman would emphasize this aspect of his situation and emotional state. Bruce Wayne misses his parents; he loves them, longs for them and considers that he has unfinished duties towards them. His capacity for love and his wish to make up for the wrong-doing perpetrated by his parents' murderer becomes even more evident with his adoption of Dick Grayson. Dick Grayson, in fact, is largely Batman's salva-tion, as Bruce Wayne emulates and becomes a version of the good father that he himself lost: his thoughts and feelings about parenthood and the nurturing relationship between parent and child now have a positive vehicle for expres-sion. Dick Grayson soon becomes Robin, and it is perhaps the character and treatment of Robin that most enable children to explore ideas about attach-ment and loss in Batman narratives in a safe and child-friendly way – at least, as child-friendly as one can get, given the subject matter.

Robin's own origin story closely parallels Batman's – only this time there is a replacement father-figure on hand in the form of Bruce Wayne. The story goes as follows. Haly's Circus is visiting Gotham City. While it is there it is subject to a protection racket: a local crime-lord, 'Boss' Tony Zucco, tells Haly to pay for 'insurance' or the safety of his circus cannot be guaranteed. The circus owner, of course, refuses to be intimidated. That night, during the show (which happens to be attended by Commissioner Gordon and Bruce Wayne) a particular act is sabotaged. The Flying Graysons – young Dick Grayson and his parents – are performing their trapeze act when one of the ropes gives way. Dick's parents plummet to their deaths. Bruce takes the distraught boy into his home at Wayne Manor, and then, as Batman, goes after Zucco, who vanishes. Some time later, when Dick has discovered Bruce's secret identity and been trained up as Robin, Zucco is rediscovered, and the two of them track him down and find the evidence that will see him face justice for the murder of Dick's parents.

Robin's Reckoning (1992), an animated version of this story for children, demonstrates very well that the emotional heart of all Batman narratives is the loss and suffering brought about by bereavement and separation. (It also demonstrates the role of Bruce Wayne's butler Alfred in many Batman stories, which is to be the moral conscience and, if need be, the emotional corrective of the piece.)

Batman: From now on, Zucco gets my undivided attention.
Alfred: How fortunate for Zucco. Because there's a little boy up there just aching for some of that attention.
Batman: I'm doing this for him!
Alfred: I'm sure revenge can be deliciously sweet; however, at the moment he needs a friend. Isn't that what you needed, Sir? [*Batman lowers his head and closes his eyes*]

. . .

Bruce: Hey, Dick; how're you doing?

Dick: Fine. [*concealing his tears*]

Bruce: Sorry I haven't been around. I forget how big and lonely this place can be.

Dick: That's okay.

Bruce: As it turns out, I may have some free time, starting tomorrow. How'd you like to catch the Gotham season opener? Box seats!

Dick: [*Without enthusiasm*] Great.

Bruce: I know it must be very difficult.

Dick: If only I could have stopped him. I saw him coming out of the tent! I knew he didn't belong there!

Bruce: I know. You keep thinking, if only I'd done something differently; if only I could have warned them. [*Stands under a giant picture of his parents*] But there isn't anything you could have done. There isn't anything *either* of us could have done.

Dick: Your mom and dad? [*Bruce nods*] Does the hurt ever go away?

Bruce: I wish I could say yes. But it will get better in time. For you. That I promise. [*Dick throws his arms around Bruce's shoulders – the first moment of closeness between them that we have seen*]

(Rogel 1992)

Bruce's comment 'You keep thinking, if only I'd done something differently' matches current understanding of real bereaved children's thinking, as discussed by Mallon (2011: 15): 'The child goes over the same ground again and again in an attempt to understand the meaning of what happened.' Mallon also discusses how bereaved children can feel guilt over having survived when their loved ones have not, and even that children 'may feel to blame for the death' (Mallon 2011: 16), something that seems evident in this dialogue between Dick and Bruce.

This particular scene shows Batman at his best, able to use the empathy that his personal grief has given him to comfort the newly-bereaved Dick Grayson. It also shows him as a *good parent and teacher:* he demonstrates understanding of the child's feelings and perspective, and he offers a reassuring manner without avoiding or dismissing the emotional hardship that he knows the child will have to go through.

Two more Batman narratives deserve particular attention with regard to this key theme of attachment, loss and grief. The first of these is the 'special' 500th issue of *Detective Comics* (1981), as it seems that the creators of this issue want to give Batman a special present to mark the occasion – they want to make everything all right for him and take his grief away. This obviously cannot be done – Batman, unlike Superman in *Superman the Movie* (1978) cannot change history to reverse the death of someone he loves – so the science-fiction device of parallel worlds is utilized. The Phantom Stranger appears and informs Batman that in one such parallel world the murder of Thomas and Martha Wayne is about to take place, and offers him the chance to prevent it:

> Phantom Stranger: The *cycle* is about to repeat itself. Thomas and Martha Wayne will *die again* – unless you *intervene*.
> Batman: *Intervene?* You mean – *travel* to this *other Earth* and *stop* the *murder?* But – *why* are you *offering* me this?
> Phantom Stranger: You're a *brave man*, Bruce Wayne . . . But despite all your *courage*, all the *good* you've done . . . you still feel you *failed* the ones you *loved* the *most*. This is your *second chance*, Bruce Wayne – and I offer it to you as a *friend* and a *comrade*.
> (Brennert and Giordano 1981: 5–6)

Needless to say, Batman accepts this second chance and is transported to the parallel Earth, accompanied by Robin (who is now a college student rather than a 10-year-old). Batman and Robin make their way to Wayne Manor to take up their protective duties and witness this world's version of young Bruce Wayne and his parents:

> Bruce Wayne: *No!* I don't *want* it! Take it *back!* [*Smashes a toy train*]
> Thomas Wayne: Your mother went to a lot of *trouble* to get you that, Bruce! I swear I've half a mind to –
> Martha Wayne: Thomas, no! It's just a *phase* he's going through!
> (Brennert and Giordano 1981: 10)

Batman and Robin's reactions to this scene are tellingly different:

> Batman: Dear Lord . . . It's as if they've *come alive* again! As if I could reach out and *touch* them again . . . *Father* . . . *Mother* . . . I *swear* by all that's *dear* to me . . . I won't let you *die again!*
> Robin: *This* Bruce Wayne is a spoiled little *brat!* I *wonder* . . . if we *stop* his *parent's murder*, will he grow up to become the *bored playboy* that Batman only *pretends* to be?
> (Brennert and Giordano 1981: 10–11)

Batman's response is really an articulation of the wish of being able to do something differently and prevent his parents' murder, but Robin's response touches upon two truly significant philosophical questions. First, to what extent does our human suffering shape our personality? Second, does our human suffering make us better people?

In much educational thought and literature there is the deeply embedded notion that learning and development should be fun and enjoyable (for example, see Phillips 1998; Woodhead 2009), but there is also an understanding that really deep learning and development are often not fun or enjoyable at all, but are borne out of overcoming cognitive or emotional difficulties and painful episodes of life (Oatley et al. 2006). Robin knows how the murder of Bruce Wayne's parents helped shape him into a force for good, albeit one in constant pain; in fact Robin's question gently invites the child reader to begin to consider why human suffering exists at all, and whether we need to experience some suffering in life in order not to be selfish or complacent over the fate and feelings of others:

> Robin: Bruce, we don't *belong* here! We have no *right* to *interfere*! Maybe every world needs a Batman!
> Batman: And what about *young Bruce*? You saw your parents *murdered* too, Dick – can you put someone else through that?
> Robin: I *am* thinking about young Bruce! We could be *condemning* him to a life as a spoiled playboy . . . and *denying* this *earth* its . . . *hero*!
> Batman: I can *appreciate* your concerns, Robin . . . but I can't *share* them. Lives are at *stake* here, including a little *boy's* life . . . a boy who'll see his family *die* before his eyes. He'll never *forget* that . . . never lose the *anger* or the *anguish*. *No one* should be *angry* all his *life*, Dick. *No one*.
>
> (Brennert and Giordano 1981: 14)

Eventually, of course, Batman and Robin do prevent the murder of this world's Thomas and Martha Wayne (with Batman saying 'This time I didn't fail them') and are transported home. The epilogue of the story shows the young Bruce Wayne of the parallel world three weeks later:

> Narrator: Martha Wayne looks at the *new books* that line Bruce's walls [*all about criminology and detection*] . . . the *new interests* that fill his life . . . and doesn't quite know what to *make* of it all.
> Martha: *Thomas*, have you noticed how *different* Bruce seems since that awful *robbery*?
> Thomas: If by *different* you mean *quieter* . . . more *studious* . . . I think it's an *improvement*. Maybe we ought to get *mugged* more often.
> Narrator: For as long as he *lives* Bruce Wayne will *remember* that night three weeks ago . . . and the *bat-winged creature* that swooped from the *sky*, saving the lives of *himself* and his *family*. *That night*, Bruce Wayne learned what *death* was . . . and he learned it could be *averted* . . . at least *temporarily*. *Years* from now, he will make a *decision* . . . choose a *direction* for his life . . . and when he does, it will not be a decision borne of *grief*, or *guilt*, or *vengeance* . . . but of *awe* . . . and *mystery* . . . and *gratitude*.
>
> (Brennert and Giordano 1981: 19)

During this narration we see young Bruce practising athletic feats. Finally, we see the boy walking home, but the shadow he casts upon the ground is that of the adult Batman. It seems that, in common with many mythical heroes (including Superman), Bruce Wayne is fated to fulfil his destiny – in this case becoming Batman no matter what – but the authors have succeeded in alleviating this particular Batman's pain and suffering and allowed him to keep his parents in his life; which is probably the only thing that Batman really wants for himself. The child reader is invited to consider the whole range of emotions mentioned at the end of the story and their impact on one's development, and the moral message of the story, essentially, is threefold: that goodness should be rewarded in kind, that suffering should be prevented and that life is sacred and should be protected and cherished.

These themes crop up again and again in Batman narratives, but one that sheds a different light on them can be found in the animated film for children, *Batman: Mask of the Phantasm* (1993). This film is set in the present, but with flashbacks to the time just before Bruce Wayne adopted the persona of Batman. The younger Bruce has, to his astonishment and surprise, fallen in love with a woman he has met, Andrea Beaumont, and finds that this has upset his plan to fulfil his vow to his dead parents. In one scene we see him trying to design what will end up being his Batman costume, disliking every design and throwing it in the fire (which is directly underneath a giant portrait of his parents):

Bruce: What am I still *doing* this for? It's got to be one or the other – I can't have it both ways. I can't put myself on the line as long as there's someone waiting for me to come home.

Alfred: Miss Beaumont would be happy to know you feel like that, Master Bruce. She's holding on line one, Sir . . . Master Bruce?

Bruce: Alfred, I can't! Not now.

Alfred: But what shall I say, Sir?

Bruce: I don't know. I just don't *know*!

(Burnett 1993)

The scene shifts to a graveyard, where a thunderstorm is taking place. We see a wet, bedraggled Bruce with his head bowed at the foot of his parents' headstone:

Bruce: It doesn't mean I don't care anymore. I don't want to let you down, honest, but – but it just doesn't *hurt* so bad anymore. You can understand that, can't you? Look; I can give money to the city, they can hire more cops, let someone else take the risk. It's *different* now!

(Burnett 1993)

A lightning flash illuminates his parents' headstone and we read the huge word *Wayne*. Bruce sinks to his knees and grasps the headstone, bowing his head:

> Bruce: *Please!* I need it to be different now. I know I made a promise, but I didn't see this coming. I didn't count on being *happy*. [*Grief-stricken voice*] Please – tell me that it's okay.
>
> Andrea: [*Appears with an umbrella*] Maybe they already have. Maybe they sent me. [*They run into each other's arms and Bruce cries on her shoulder*]
>
> (Burnett 1993)

This episode shows the adult Bruce still needing the approval of his dead parents – something that has an extra edge because of the fervent promise he made to them at the time of their deaths. This illustrates the 'continuing bonds' model of responses to bereavement, which is when bereaved children continue to include their lost ones in their subsequent lives. This is explained by Mallon (2011: 15) as follows: 'Children . . . think about what their dead parent or sibling would advise them to do or behave in a way the deceased would approve of.' Bruce needs his dead parents' permission to break his promise to them. He says 'It's different now', but his subsequent statement 'Please! I need it to be different now' clearly demonstrates that, actually, it is not different at all; that Bruce's pain and suffering are just as fresh and present as they have always been, which is, perhaps, why he finds it very odd to be, because of his developing relationship with Andrea, 'happy'. The device of having Bruce talk to his dead parents is not just for the benefit of the viewer's understanding of his feelings either; Hermans et al. (1992: 28) suggested that we all engage in a version of such dialogues with those we love and whose opinions we care for: 'Imaginal dialogues play a central role in our daily lives: They exist alongside actual dialogues with real others and, interwoven with actual interactions, they constitute an essential part of our narrative construction of the world.' Andrea's suggestion 'Maybe they have, maybe they sent me' is a lovely and generous attempt to allow Bruce to tell himself a story of his life that would include a notion that his dead parents would give him their blessing if he gave up trying to keep his promise and set up a new life with Andrea instead. In fact, what we really want for Bruce Wayne at this point is for him to give up all this pre-Batman preparation and fixation, go off and marry Andrea (and perhaps have children with her) and finally become a happy man. Sadly, though, it is not to be.

So Batman and his narratives can be understood as explorations of attachment, loss and grief and the effects of these on the person, but also as explorations of that person's attempt to respond positively to the attachment needs of others. This is true even of the Batman stories produced for the youngest of his readers; for example, the whole dynamic of *Help Wanted* (2012) is that Batman prevents a man from continuing with crime in order to ward off the family breakdown that would follow as a result of his eventual imprisonment. Batman ends the story by talking with the now reformed and productively employed man's wife and son: 'I don't often get the opportunity to give someone a *second chance* instead of just locking him away. But, after all – no boy should have to grow up without a *father*' (Fisch 2012: 26).

The key moral consideration that emerges from this element of Batman narratives is the importance of compassion and the moral imperative to prevent or alleviate suffering – especially suffering related to attachment and loss. This in itself would make Batman narratives worth engaging with for children, but there is another dimension to them too – one that is, perhaps, more disturbing.

Batman, immorality, amorality and evil

The key villains whom Batman regularly encounters are, perhaps, the most genuinely worrying villains in the entirety of superhero narratives – at least in the versions of them aimed at readers and viewers over 12 years of age. They seem to represent the darkest aspects of what humanity is capable of, and they illustrate different types of malice, hatred, contempt for others, abdication of moral responsibility, arrogance and brutality. Many of them are periodically imprisoned in what can only be described as a cesspit of a penal institution, Arkham Asylum (whose name itself suggests a strong connection between wrongdoing and evil and mental illness or madness).

First, there are the more obviously thuggish and physically brutal foes like Killer Croc, Amygdala and Bane, a 'primarily physical villain with a sort of monstrous aspect' (Nolan, quoted by Roberts 2012: 22) who is currently on display in *The Dark Knight Rises* (2012) and who famously broke Batman's back in *Batman: Knightfall* (Moench 1993). Such villains dominate and crush any opposition to their self-centred attempts to develop wealth and power-bases through sweeping and brutal use of threat and violence, or are employed by others with more of a concern for their clean public image. These villains use physical intimidation and brute force to get their way, and are akin to the classroom bullies that children might be unfortunate enough to encounter. The moral issue raised here is the use of power to oppress. (In Bane's case there is also the issue of how poor circumstances can corrupt one's moral outlook: in some stories Bane attempts to visit the brutality that he was brought up in on the rest of the world.)

Then there are villains with causes; for example, Catwoman (who seeks to promote the welfare of animals – especially of any types of cat – and punish any who mistreat them) and Poison Ivy (who similarly regards the plant kingdom as much better than the human one and plant life as more valuable than human). Perhaps the most significant villain here is Ra's Al Ghul, who helped train Bruce Wayne on his way to becoming Batman in *Batman Begins* (Nolan 2005), but was deceptive about his purpose. Ra's al Ghul is actually involved in trying to mould the world to fit his own vision of what would constitute the desired good for all or greater good (see Chapter 8) – but, just like Jarvis Kord in *Fall of the Blue Beetle!* (2010), this involves the removal of all freedom for anyone else. Ra's explains:

> I am neither a zealot nor a madman. I am a realist at least and a futurist at best. Some do not agree. Thus, we must use whatever means necessary to protect and preserve what mankind would pillage and rape. The world will thank us someday.
>
> (Wagner 2003: 11)

Unfortunately this mission involves things such as attempting to destroy what he regards as the decadent and impure Gotham City and other parts of the world through terrorist acts and the assassination of people he deems incompatible with the realization of his vision.

The moral issue here is that of the veracity of the whole notion of any 'greater good', who gets to decide and authorize what any greater good is, and what actions are allowed or disallowed morally in trying to achieve any vision of a greater good (in other words, whether 'by any means necessary' is a viable moral position to take). This is a real-life moral issue, as, for example, most actual terrorist groups claim some vision of the world that, for them, is more desirable than the present actuality, and which, they claim, gives them moral authority to carry out their acts of terrorism. For children, dealing with questions about Ra's Al Ghul and his actions is less worrying than dealing with, say Al Qaeda or animal rights terrorists or people such as Anders Behring Breivik (and so on) because these groups and individuals cause real death, damage and suffering in the world in the service of their respective causes, while Ra's Al Ghul and other like villains remain fictional.

Batman also has to face villains who have, like him, suffered some dreadful trauma or loss, but use their personal tragedies to justify their subsequent criminal behaviour towards others. Mr Freeze (real name, Dr. Victor Fries) is notable here, as his whole motivation derives from his suffering over the situation of his wife, Nora, who is terminally ill and cryogenically frozen. As well as committing crimes to fund attempts to cure his wife, Mr Freeze pursues those he deems responsible for his wife's situation – which is very similar to Batman's pursuit of the man responsible for his parents' murder, except for the lengths to which Mr Freeze is willing to go: he is quite prepared to kill those he holds to blame and is quite careless about who else might get hurt along the way. The moral issue raised here is justice versus vengeance and what differentiates and separates the two. Batman has moral boundaries that are not shared by Mr Freeze, and the reader is invited to consider what moral boundaries might be appropriate and why.

Another opponent of Batman who has suffered personal loss and trauma is Harvey Dent, now Two-Face. Dent was an honest and incorruptible district attorney who had acid thrown in his face during a trial. The resulting scarring deformed half of his face and, it seems, affected his mind. Dent then decided that as well as having a dual face (and soon dual clothing) he also had a dual morality, half good and half evil, and that it was completely down to chance which of these won out. Two-Face carries a two-headed dollar coin, one side of which is scarred, and flips this coin to decide whether he will perform a good action or an evil one. The moral issue raised is that of moral responsibility and whether a person can actually abdicate his own moral responsibility and leave good and evil to chance or not. Two-Face often talks about how, in his opinion at least, whether we end up performing good or evil actions is simply a matter of chance and happenstance.

Finally, there are the very frightening villains who seem quite pathological in nature. The Scarecrow (the psychologist Jonathan Crane) develops a 'psychology of terror' (Cotta Vaz 1989: 159) and operates by using a fear toxin to paralyse his victims with their deepest fears, often killing them along the way or subjecting them to a subsequent lifetime of nightmare and trauma. The motive for this seems to be that he revels in people's fear and terror. This makes him a pertinent counterpoint to Batman, who, of course, wants to strike terror into criminals' hearts, but for different reasons. The moral issues raised are the relationship between motive and choice of behaviour and whether or not the level of goodness of an action changes depending on whom the action is aimed at. (This is a key issue of all superhero narratives, of course, because superheroes do use violence: does it make a difference that their violence is aimed at wrongdoers and is often intended to ward off poor, unjust and undesirable consequences?)

The final villain who deserves some discussion is the Joker – perhaps the most maniacal and frightening villain of them all. The Joker leaves his victims with a trademark rictus on their faces, which makes them appear as if they are smiling, whether or not they are actually terrified or even dead. He also uses a laughing gas that makes his victims unable to stop laughing – possibly for ever – and leaves a playing-card joker by his victims as his literal calling-card. He strikes at people and things seemingly on a whim, or because they irritate or frustrate him, and he seems to have no regard for the number or the relative innocence of people he hurts. He also seems completely obsessed with Batman, as if he were incomplete without the presence of Batman in his world, and is the moral opposite of him when it comes to his goals:

> While the Dark Knight and his allies strive to protect the people of Gotham, the Joker seeks to kill, maim and torture them. The two are

at war and are, in many ways, the antithesis that defines each other's existence.

(Cowsill 2012: 12)

He is, in other words, dangerous and deranged, and there is no real explanation offered to rationalize why – he just is. It is, perhaps, this lack of explanation for his existence but his existence nonetheless that is most deeply troubling (as well as the level of irrational, unpredictable and indiscriminate danger that he poses, of course).

The moral issue raised by the Joker is what actions are allowed in response to such a man. White (2008: 5) asks 'Why doesn't Batman kill the Joker?', and suggests as part of his discussion that:

> The argument in favour of killing the Joker is fairly straightforward – if Batman kills the Joker, he would prevent all the murders the Joker would otherwise commit in the future . . . Saving many lives at the cost of just one would represent a net increase in well-being.
>
> (White 2008: 7)

But, of course, Batman will not kill, and has an abhorrence of killing because of what happened to him and his parents. The moral principle 'thou shalt not kill' is, for Batman, absolute and non-negotiable, regardless of circumstances. As Superman remarks: 'More than anyone else in the world, when you scratch everything else away from Batman, you're left with someone who doesn't want to see anybody die' (Waid and Ross 2008: 151). So the moral issue raised by the Joker is also whether moral principles (such as 'thou shalt not kill') are set in stone or whether their applicability depends on the situation at hand – an approach to morality known as *moral relativism*. This is a big question for children who are routinely instructed, for example, to be honest and not to lie, but find themselves in situations where telling the truth as they understand it will lead to undesirable or even distressing consequences (recall from Chapter 4 the example of the boy who thought a girl in his class was fat), or instructed not to use violence when their every instinct tells them that one well-landed punch on the bully's nose will stop the bully from picking on them ever again.

It is worth noting, of course, that younger children's engagement with Batman's villains is much gentler and lighter than the above discussion might indicate. For the younger children the villains are much more defined by their visual appearance and gadgets than they are by the emotional or moral situations. Even the Joker, the most worrying villain of all, is tempered and diffused for younger children; he is presented as more of a trickster and a practical joker, and he is often accompanied by a comic female companion with a funny voice called Harley Quinn, who calls him 'Pudding' and 'Mr J', and who is frequently the cause of his being involved in what is essentially slapstick humour. A key way that younger children explore Batman's villains is, after all, through the digital games *Lego Batman* (TT Games Publishing 2008) and its successor *Lego Batman 2: DC Super Heroes* (TT Games Publishing 2012), which are inherently funny and ridiculous, and the delight of these games is to make virtual Lego constructions that allow things to happen and work out how to progress up levels rather than engage in anything with emotional depth.

Even so, children involved in this game and other simple Batman narratives are beginning their exploration of something potentially much deeper. As compelling as his costume, gadgets, vehicles, movement and presence as Batman are, the most telling narratives of Batman are ones which involve his humanity surfacing and which shed light on the moral dimensions of his ongoing task to avenge evil. Without this humanity he might be a two-dimensional character with little of interest or substance to offer children, but as it is, the human tempering of his mission makes his characters and stories capable of resonating deeply; children are offered the opportunity to explore human motivations, emotions, moral choices and the consequences of loss and grief on people's well-being – and to do so from the safe distance of being a reader or viewer of fictional narratives that are not directly about *them*.

Learning ideas

As with Superman, Batman and his narratives can be utilized in teaching opportunities – but probably with older children if the particular characteristics discussed above are to be utilized. These opportunities are very much related to Ethics, PSHE and Citizenship and Philosophy in the first instance, with further potential for use of the character in Design and Technology, Art, and English and Drama. Batman also has scope to be used with child development students or trainee teachers or counsellors, particularly, of course, with regard to attachment theory. This section presents a list of possible prompts.

Design a thematic superhero

Batman takes his iconography from bats, with his cape and cowl, for example. After perusing examples of Batman artwork, children could be invited to design their own creature-related superheroes (such as Tiger-Girl, Eagleboy or Sharkman) and design their appearance and equipment to evoke aspects of the creatures after which they are named. An extension of this would be for children to create origin stories for their own superheroes that connected them somehow to the creatures in their names.

Design a hideout for a superhero

Batman has a very distinctive and visually appropriate headquarters in the Batcave. Children could design their own thematic hideouts to complement the superheroes that they have previously created.

Batman's moral principles

We know that Batman will not kill, and that he values life. Children could explore selected Batman narratives to see what other moral principles they might be able to identify. They could then draw up their own personal lists of moral principles and give reasons for them or examples of how they might be put into practice in real life. An extension of this would be to explore where several of society's key moral principles come from and find expression in different cultures (for example, the Ten Commandments).

Another extension of this for older children would be to explore the whole notion of moral relativism and ask children to decide whether there would be any circumstances in which Batman would be justified in not applying his key moral principles. They could be given prompts for this, for example: would Batman be justified in killing the Joker if the world was safer as a result – as White (2008) suggests? One way of structuring the lesson would be to get the children to create stories which involved Batman facing such a moral choice – stories which could either be written down or dramatized. A good extension for this last option would be to get children to dramatize *both* possible choices (for example, deciding to kill the Joker and deciding not to kill him) and explore what consequences arise as a result of each possible course of action.

Resilience and determination (1)

Batman does not have any superpowers; instead he trained himself from an early age to become the crime-fighter he is today. He developed physical skills, academic knowledge and the ability to think deductively. Children could be offered this example, then asked to consider any long-term aim that they have or are considering. They could discuss and record ideas of how they would prepare their own bodies and minds, and what they would study to achieve these aims.

Resilience and determination (2)

Bruce Wayne did not let the loss of his parents stop him from pursuing his goal. Children could consider any common goals they might share as a class and what difficulties or anxieties might impede their progress towards these goals. They could identify ways they could help each other at moments when any of these anticipated or worried-about difficulties emerge. These ways of helping could be recorded and a 'Batman Award for Determination' could be given out to children who stick at it and overcome difficulties, and a 'Batman Award for Being a Good Friend' could be given out to children who help others overcome their difficulties.

The bereaved boy

Bruce Wayne is orphaned at an early age. Children could be asked to imagine that they were friends with the young Bruce Wayne, and how they could help him and look after him. Student teachers and other trainee professionals could be asked the same question, only this time imagining themselves in their future professional roles rather than as friends to Bruce. Such students could also view *Batman: Mask of the Phantasm* (1993) – considered above – and discuss how best to support adults who have suffered bereavement.

Justice versus vengeance

After exploring selected narratives involving Batman and Mr Freeze, children could be involved in dramatizing a meeting between them with each party expressing his own point of view about how to respond to the hurt and crime against him. This could be developed further in several ways once the basic framework of the scene had been established: children could write a script for the scene; they could plot or write the story of what happened before the two characters meet, or what will happen next; they could decide to what extent they want any audience of the scene to sympathize with either Batman or Mr Freeze, and work out ways to direct and play the scene accordingly.

Is mankind good or evil?

Older children could read the story *Evil in Paradise* in *World's Finest Comics #222* (Haney et al. 1974, discussed in Chapter 2, and currently available in Haney and Dillin 2008) which is the story that has the elder Superman and Batman telling their sons that mankind is respectively good and evil. They could then be introduced to basic versions of different models of childhood, for example: Rousseau's notion that children are born pure, innocent, close to nature and essentially good; the Puritan notion that children are representatives of a flawed species and, therefore, like all the rest of humanity, are prone to evil and wickedness; and Locke's notion that human beings are born as 'blank slates', neither naturally good nor evil, but dependent on the influence of the outside world. Children could explore the origin story of Batman and discuss how the influence of the outside world has affected his character, and whether he was born good or made good by having to deal with his situation. They could then consider the same question with regard to themselves.

11 The X-Men: the rejected group in society

The X-Men characters provide an opportunity for children to explore ideas about rejection, fear, prejudice, equality, inclusion and standing up for one's rights.

Introduction

> Nightcrawler: I am so sick of *hiding*, Peter.
>
> Colossus: I do not think the world is ready for us yet, Tovarisch. We must be *patient* –
>
> Nightcrawler: I have been 'patient' all my *life*. What I saw today – what I *felt* – makes me wonder if there is any *point* to this place – they wanted me *dead*. What hope is there for me when the mere sight of my *face* ignites such *hatred*? What hope is there for *any* of us?
>
> *Refuge* (Gray 2012: 11)

There are several well-established groups of superheroes (such as the Fantastic Four, the Justice League and the Avengers), but perhaps the most popular and significant of these is the X-Men. The X-Men characters and narratives raise and explore a specific set of important moral issues in a very focused and deliberate manner, as this chapter will demonstrate. This team of superheroes and the nature of the world they inhabit are different from all others in two major ways: the range of peoples represented by the various characters who constitute the X-Men at different times, and the fact that they (and many of their frequent opponents) are part of a wider minority group that are feared, misunderstood and even hated by the world that surrounds them for simply being what they are. More than any other superheroes, the X-Men exist in an uneasy relationship with the rest of the world, and the moral questions raised by X-Men narratives are ones about intolerance, inclusion, and how best to respond if one finds oneself and one's group rejected by others.

This moral focus is made possible by the fact that the X-Men are designated as being 'mutants'. This decision seems to have started life as a plot device; it neatly and economically accounted for the existence of the various powers and abilities that different X-Men had (just as Spider-Man, the Hulk and the Fantastic Four all owe their particular abilities to exposure to radiation in some manner). As early as *X-Men #1* (1963), however, even more creative and thought-provoking possibilities of this decision begin to be explored. Mutation is put forward *à la* Charles Darwin as an evolutionary process, with the logical result that the 'mutants' referred to in the comics represent the next step of human evolution. They are, therefore, to some extent a group apart, and the comics, films and animated television series that follow all explore the wary and sometimes destructive relationship between the mutants and the non-mutants. The theme is really the extent to which common humanity exists between the two groups and what moral duties they owe to one another. The back-cover blurb for *X-Men Ultimate Collection* (2011) which collects the whole of the children's 1990s animated *X-Men* television series together, illustrates this nicely:

> Born into a world that fears and distrusts them, mutants struggle for equality with humans. The X-Men believe it is a battle worth fighting for. But while some mutants work for peace, others wage a secret war to eliminate humans and seize power for themselves . . . Feared and hated by the world they have sworn to protect, these are the strangest heroes of all! The uncanny X-Men!
>
> (Lewald 2011)

Children engaging with the X-Men are drawn into very edgy narratives that explore good and not so good but possibly understandable responses to being 'feared and hated'. The stories evoke what it feels like to be rejected and explore ways in which rejected and sometimes oppressed people (and peoples) can respond in turn. This makes the X-Men very useful as a resource for engaging children with many historical and ethical issues, as will be seen.

Professor Xavier's School for Gifted Youngsters: the inclusive family

The leader of the X-Men is Professor Charles Xavier (a telepath), who runs a very plush learning academy. This had had several names and been in several locations over the years, but the most canonical and familiar of these is *Professor Xavier's School for Gifted Youngsters*, set in a fine mansion in its own grounds in Westchester, New York. This is, significantly, a genuine school rather than just a cover for X-Men operations (though it is their headquarters too), and the 'gifts' that Professor X nurtures are, of course, mutations; the school is partly designed to help young people become accomplished at living with and controlling their mutant powers, and, most importantly, using these powers properly and for Good. (Rather tellingly, when we see part of a typical lesson in the film *X-Men: The Last Stand* (Ratner 2006) the subject of the lesson is 'mutant ethics'.) The adult members of the X-Men are all tutors at the school (even the ferocious and anti-social Wolverine who leads the younger scholars in battle and teamwork scenarios, and who, in the film *X2: X-Men United* (Singer 2003) rather dryly describes himself to young Bobby 'Iceman' Drake's parents as a 'professor of art'), and there is an explicit concern shown for the upbringing of the next generation and the overarching aim to establish peace and harmonious co-existence between mutants and non-mutant humans through the ambassadorship of the students at the school in their future lives. Importantly (and quite differently from Magneto's Brotherhood of Mutants, as will be seen below), the X-Men operate in the service of all, both mutant and non-mutant humans alike, and work for what they see as the greater good for everyone, not just for their fellow mutants (or others of their particular ethnic group, if you like).

Very fittingly, given the themes of acceptance and rejection that pervade the X-Men narratives, the composition of this group is, perhaps, the most inclusive and diverse of any superhero group. Within its adult membership at various different times we find the following (among others): Professor X himself, who is disabled and wheelchair-bound; the Cairo-born and Kenya-raised African-American Ororo Munroe (Storm), whom Professor X has in mind for his successor in *X-Men: The Last Stand* (2006); the Bavarian Kurt Wagner (Nightcrawler), a deeply religious man who suffered persecution before coming to America; Scott Summers (Cyclops), who was orphaned as a boy; the Siberian Piotr Rasputin (Colossus), who helped his local community fight against state oppression; the Irish Sean Cassidy (Banshee); the astonishingly powerful Jean Grey (later Phoenix); the French Remy LeBeau (Gambit); the Japanese Hisako Ichiki (Armor); the Canadian James Logan Howlett (Wolverine); and another Canadian, Jean-Paul Beaubier (Northstar), who proposed to and married his boyfriend Kyle Jinadu in *Astonishing X-Men #51* (2004), one of the covers of which featured the couple in a full-blown kiss and embrace. There are also the student members of the X-Men, such as the Jewish Kitty Pryde (Ariel), the Chinese-American Jubilation Lee (Jubilee), Anna Marie (Rogue), Bobby Drake (Iceman), and, in some depictions, Warren Worthington III (Angel), all of whom are typically portrayed as younger and more vulnerable (but not necessarily less powerful) people who look up to the adults in the group to mentor, guide and take care of them.

Of particular note are the women of the X-Men, who are consistently among the most powerful and effective women in any superhero narratives. Dr Jean Grey, who was specially recruited by Professor X, is not only a telekinetic and telepath whose ability threatens to eclipse Professor X's own, and a strong and articulate leader and ambassador for mutants in her own right (including representing mutant rights causes to the American Senate), but also, in her personality as the Phoenix, almost an elemental force of nature with very little limitation to her power. The independently wealthy Emma Frost (the White Queen) leads her own influential organization (the Hellfire Club) and follows her own agenda, working with and as part of the X-Men only when she chooses to. She is another powerful telepath, and can transform her body into diamond. Ororo Munroe (Storm) can control the very weather itself, but her importance is more that both the younger and older members of the X-Men look up to her for consistently sound and well-articulated moral guidance. Ororo acts as a mentor to many of the others, particularly the much younger Kitty Pryde (whose name is a playful version of *female pride*), who can move through walls and other solid objects. Most depictions of the X-Men are composed of a more or less equal ratio of men and women, and the women of the group are consistently shown as having a hugely strong, confident, and morally informed impact on any group decisions that are arrived at. Any girls engaging with the X-Men will find powerful female role models on display throughout.

All of this means that the X-Men serve as an excellent exemplar of an inclusive and collaborative community. Its members represent a range of ethnic and social groups, different nationalities, both genders, people of different sexual orientations, and people of different ages and with different needs all combining together as one large cohesive unit in the service of their principles and mission. They operate rather like a large family, but, as Fingeroth (2004: 108–109) observes:

> Where the mutant family differs from the everyday family, is that their very being together is the result of and in service to a higher purpose . . . It's a fantasy about finding your real family. It's you and them against the world. No matter how much you bicker and fight, they're the ones who will protect you, as you will them.

The different personalities contained within the group, plus the various plot-lines that lead to love-triangles, jealousies, misunderstandings, disagreements, and so on, mean that the behaviour of different members of the team towards one another is often edgy and confrontational, but all these various difficulties are always put to one side when it comes to the team working effectively together for the common cause and the greater good, often articulated for the benefit of the reader or viewer by Charles Xavier, who is the steadfast moral compass of the group: 'I never asked for an easy life', he tells his friend-and-enemy Eric Lensherr (Magneto) on one occasion, 'only a just one' (Lewald 2011). The team stand as a vision of what is possible within human communities when they are well motivated and have an inclusive and respectful attitude towards their own members.

The establishment of the X-Men around Professor Xavier's School for Gifted Youngsters is important for another reason too, as it symbolizes the whole perpetual parental and educational mission of bringing up the next generation to be good people who act well towards themselves and each other. As Evans (2005: 172) notes:

> We can certainly imagine that Xavier reflects an upbringing that nurtured a love in him for the good . . . An important aspect of Xavier's school for mutants is that it is a place where the students can be accepted and loved, and thus naturally come to desire to be like those who are dedicated to helping them.

This is what many real-life teachers and parents wish to make happen: they work in the hope that their good example and caring behaviour, in combination with their good words about how to treat one's own self and others, will rub off on the children they nurture through life. A great part of the X-Men's value is that they live their principles about inclusion, acceptance and care for others rather than just pay lip-service to them. Their stories show them caring for others and accepting and valuing other people for who they are, as well as just talking about the importance of these things. It is perhaps this above all that makes the X-Men good moral role models.

Unfortunately, however, the inhabitants of the world outside the walls of Professor Xavier's School for Gifted Youngsters do not see things that way.

Feared and hated by the world

In the X-Men's universe the growing phenomenon of human mutation is met with fear, distrust and hatred on the part of 'normal' humans. These utterly negative responses manifest themselves in different, but always grim ways.

First of all, there are the confusion, shame and rejection shown by parents of mutant children; for example, in the children's animated *X-Men* television series of the 1990s, young Jubilation Lee's parents share this exchange:

> Jubilee's mother: But how could you register her with that Mutant Control Agency as if she was some sort of criminal?
>
> Jubilee's father: The Agency isn't a prison, Martha, it's an outreach programme to help these unfortunate people. It's for her own good. You know I love her.
>
> Jubilee's mother: But what will happen to her now?

Jubilee's father: I don't know. Let's just hope the neighbours never find out our beautiful Jubilee is a mutant. They'd never understand.

(Edens 1992)

Similarly, in the film *X2: X-Men United* (2003), Bobby Drake's mother asks him if he has ever tried *not* to be mutant, while in *X-Men: The Last Stand* (2006), Warren Worthington II, who dislikes and fears mutants intensely, attempts to coerce his son, Warren Worthington III (Angel), to take what he believes is a cure for his mutation. These things, of course, have echoes of parents authorizing treatment on their children at different points in history to combat 'conditions' such as homosexuality – as dramatized by Jeanette Winterson in *Oranges Are Not the Only Fruit* (1985/2001) – or even, more recently, contested disorders such as ADHD. Warren Worthington II takes even more drastic measures with his son in the children's animated television series *Wolverine and the X-Men* (2008) by authorizing the amputation of his son's wings without his permission and while he is unconscious. Other mutant children are abandoned or given up for adoption, and so on. (A key moral issue raised by these scenarios is, of course, that of children's rights, and the whole question of who gets to decide what actions are in children's best interests: the adults responsible for the children's upbringing and welfare or the children themselves.)

Children presented with these scenes can see that rejection by one's parents hurts, and can wonder how any morality of care (see Chapter 4) can be present. Surely if one of the moral maxims laid down by the Ten Commandments is 'honour thy father and thy mother', then this should be a reciprocal duty? Many of the parents depicted in X-Men stories demonstrate a mixture of love for their children and revulsion against a key part of their identity.

Secondly, there is the active verbal and physical abuse and violent behaviour that is often meted out to those suspected of being mutants by the people around them. We often see people vocalizing or using placards or signs that use expressions such as 'No Muties Here!' and gangs of men beating up those they consider to be mutants and smashing their property. When Wolverine's mutation is revealed early on in the film *X-Men* (2000), the owner of the bar he is in orders him to get out. Many other X-Men, particularly Nightcrawler, have suffered violent persecution for being mutants. Newscasters and politicians frequently refer to anti-mutant hysteria or the 'mutant threat' that somehow imperils society.

This idea of a 'mutant threat' is taken up by several politicians and military leaders. Senator Kelly is a character who recurs in several versions of the X-Men, and who serves to give voice to the desire to control mutants and alleviate any potential threat that they might offer. Early in the film *X-Men* (2000) we see Kelly address a Senate hearing that is being held to decide whether or not all mutants should be registered and accounted for:

Kelly: Three words: Are mutants dangerous?

Jean Grey: Senator, it is a fact that mutants who've come forward and revealed themselves publically have been met with fear, hostility, even violence. It is because of that ever present hostility that I am urging the Senate to vote against mutant registration. To force mutants to expose themselves would only—

Kelly: Expose themselves? What is it the mutant community has to hide, I wonder, that makes them so afraid to identify themselves?

Jean Grey: I didn't say they were hiding.

Kelly: Well, let me show you what is being hidden, Miss Grey. I have here a list of names of identified mutants living right here in the United States. We have a girl in Illinois who can walk through walls. Now, what's to stop her walking into a bank vault, or the White House, or into their houses [*gesturing to the onlookers*]? There are even rumours, Miss Grey, of mutants so powerful that they can enter our minds and control our thoughts [which is exactly what Professor X can do] taking away our God-given free will. I think the American people deserve the right to decide whether their children should go to school with mutants, to be taught by mutants. Ladies and gentlemen, the truth is that mutants are very real, and they are among us. We must know who they are, and, above all, we must know what they can do.

(Singer 2000)

As well as the obvious stoking of fear and paranoia, this speech has quite deliberate echoes of the racial segregation that the American civil rights movement fought so hard to overcome, and also speaks to other more current forms of prejudice, such as what seems to be growing anti-Muslim sentiment in the West (Talwar 2012). Kelly is advocating separatism and control. Later in the film, in the following exchange with Mystique, who has been disguised as one of his aides, we get a hint of what Kelly's world-view leads to in practice for anyone at the receiving end of it:

Kelly: If it was up to me, I'd lock 'em all away. It's a war. It's the reason why people like me exist.

Mystique: You know, people like you is the reason I was afraid to go to school as a child.

(Singer 2000)

The entire idea of the wholesale registration of a people, as proposed by Kelly, is rightly resisted by the X-Men; but it is Eric Lensherr (Magneto) who accurately critiques it to Charles Xavier in *X-Men: First Class* (Vaughan 2011): 'Identification – that's how it starts – and ends with being rounded up, experimented on, eliminated.' Lensherr should know, as he is from a Jewish family who suffered exactly these things under the Nazis when he was a boy. In fact, the parallel between the fate suffered by the Jews in the Holocaust and the situation that the mutants of the world see looming for them is emphasized in many X-Men narratives, not least because Magneto's approach to dealing with what he understands as the human threat to mutants stems precisely from the appalling oppression and destruction he and his Jewish family suffered at the hands of the Nazis (see below).

One particularly effective expression of this parallel is found in the children's animated television series *Wolverine and the X-Men* (2008), and is worth exploring simply because it is aimed precisely at child viewers. To give a flavour of it: each episode's opening credits and many scenes throughout the series feature huge red-and-purple robots patrolling the streets searching for mutants. These are the Sentinels, anti-mutant constructs who have appeared in many X-Men narratives since 1965 and whose mission is 'to serve and protect', which translates in practice as 'to serve and protect humans by removing and destroying mutants'. A parallel between the Sentinels and the Nazis' treatment of Jews was identified by DeFalco (2008: 110):

> Both Stan Lee and Jack Kirby had served in World War II and were familiar with the Nazi military organization called the Schtzstaffel, or, as it was better known, the SS. This elite military unit rounded up political prisoners and sent them off to the concentration camps. There can be little doubt that Lee and Kirby had the SS in mind when they introduced the Sentinels in *The X-Men #14* . . . Their mission was to protect humanity's genetic purity by capturing and subduing all mutants.

At the same time, back in the opening credits, we see the heavily armoured storm-troopers of the government-authorized 'Mutant Response Department' seeking out mutants by smashing in their doors, capturing them and rounding them up in armoured vehicles. The most telling part of the credits shows two young and terrified children in their night attire running from the stormtroopers. The scene is partly shown through the stormtroopers' enhanced goggles, which have the word 'MUTANT' superimposed over the children, to make clear exactly why they are being hunted down – at least, until the furious form of Wolverine interposes himself between the children and their hunter, with the last part of this scene being Wolverine's fist thrusting towards the goggles. Wolverine – and, by extension, the rest of the X-Men – are introduced as protectors of the weak, vulnerable, innocent and persecuted.

One notable detail of this scene stands out. There are no patterns or pictures on the children's pyjamas save one: the little boy's pyjamas feature a large yellow star in the centre of the chest. This is not exactly the Jewish Star of David as used by the Nazis to identify those who could be victimized and persecuted with the blessing of the state (as that would be too blatant, and possibly too limiting, as the X-Men's situation stands as a metaphor for that of any systematically oppressed group), but it is very close, and the parallel between the persecution of the mutants and that of the Jews under Hitler is made explicit, clear and deliberate.

As the series unfolds, we discover that the world depicted in the credits is the future world, and the X-Men's job is to ensure that this particular future never happens. A key plot device sees the Charles Xavier from this future communicating frequently with the Wolverine of the present day, which guides the child viewer through moral and emotional decisions and choices of behaviour made by various humans, the X-Men themselves, Magneto and his Brotherhood of Mutants (see below) in the present, and also the likely consequences of these actions, decisions and feelings in the future. All the while, the whole range of characters – from Colonel Moss and Senator Kelly, who hate and fear mutants, and Warren Worthington II, who thinks mutants are sufferers of a medical condition, to Magneto, who regards humanity as an enemy and a threat that must be destroyed, and the X-Men themselves, who work for peaceful co-existence, respect and equal rights – give voice to what motivates them, and children are given a safe vehicle for exploring fear, prejudice and hatred, but also hope, equality and love.

Perhaps the key and most articulate X-Men narrative of all time (Garrett 2005) is Chris Claremont's *God Loves, Man Kills* (1982/2007), which serves to bring home the entire moral content of all X-Men stories. This story involves a group who title themselves the Purifiers and whose self-declared mission, as this name suggests, is to preserve what they see as the purity of the human race – something which echoes the Nazis' philosophy, but also all the incidences of 'ethnic cleansing' found in older and more recent history the world over. The Purifiers are led in secret by the Bible-quoting television evangelist, Reverend William Stryker. The danger from Stryker, like that of many charismatic evil men before him, is that he adopts a personable public style that seems to consist of reasonableness itself, and that he articulates his argument skilfully and with a confidence and conviction that sway many members of the public.

The story begins, horribly, with the Purifiers' murder of two young children and their parents for being mutants. Then we see young Kitty Pryde involved in a fight with a youth the same age:

Danny: I was talkin' about the Stryker crusade [*a carefully chosen word*], an' all the good it does. My folk an' I are members, what's wrong with that?

Kitty: Tell her the rest, creep – about how Reverend Stryker's gonna save humanity – from the godless hordes of *mutantkind*!

Danny: Well, he is! Muties are evil! They deserve whatever they get! You wanna make something of it, mutie-lover?!

(Claremont 1982/2007: 122)

The fight is broken up by Stevie Hunter, a neighbour of them both (who happens to be black):

> Stevie: C'mon, let's get you inside and cleaned up.
> Kitty: How can you be so *calm*?! Didn't you hear what he said?
> Stevie: They're only words, child.
> Kitty: Suppose he'd called me a *nigger*-lover, Stevie?! Would you be so damn' tolerant then?!!
>
> (Claremont 1982/2007: 122)

This exchange serves to evoke the low-level but deeply harmful bullying that can exist in real children's lives, and how racist and other dismissive name-calling and rejection of whole groups of people can hurt. It also suggests that the character Danny sees no harm in what he is doing. There is considerable scope here for exploring this issue further in Citizenship: the difference between good-natured teasing and hateful bullying, and why the vocabulary people use matters.

Part of the story shows a television debate between Stryker and Professor Xavier:

> Xavier: Mutants per se are not a monolithic group, possessing one set of attitudes or goals. They are individuals – as are we all – and should be judged as such.
> Stryker: Now there you go, Charles. These 'individuals' possess some pretty terrifying powers. How are we common folk going to defend ourselves against them? . . . After all, Charles, is it fair to even call mutants 'human'? The generic term for them is, I believe, Homo Superior – which relates to a different species altogether.
>
> (Claremont 1982/2007: 125)

Several of the X-Men are watching this debate on television:

> Wolverine: Take Stryker's remark about mutants not bein' human to its ultimate an' we've no rights under the law. No rights to *have* any rights. Or protection.
> Rogue: It seems impossible, but Stryker's so popular. Millions of people believe his every word.
> Colossus: To think us evil, simply because we exist? It is madness.
> Nightcrawler: I have known such fear and hatred from birth – but time does not make it any easier to take.
>
> (Claremont 1982/2007: 126)

The themes raised here could be explored by children in relation to many issues that arise in the subjects History, Citizenship and Ethics. We have the issue of whether it is proper to use group categories to define people at all, or whether it is individual character, belief and action that matter. We have the issue of rights granted to people under the law (or not granted). We have the reminder that approaches such as Stryker's are manifestations of fear, hatred and rejection, regardless of how reasonable the tone of voice used to communicate them is. Children could look at real-life charismatic and dictatorial leaders (especially Hitler) and their policies and ask questions about why policies full of hate become popular in certain conditions.

As the story progresses we find out that Stryker, in fact, regards mutants not only as less than human but as creations of the Devil:

> Storm: We have done you no harm – why are you doing this?
> Stryker: Because you exist. And that existence is an affront to the Lord . . .
> The Lord created man and woman in *His* image, blessed with His grace.
> Mutants broke that sacred mold. They were creations, not of God, but
> of the *Devil*. And *I* had been chosen to lead the fight against them.
> (Claremont 1982/2007: 145–147)

As well as demonstrating hubris by setting himself up as the chosen one of God, Stryker indulges in perpetual and selective quoting from the Bible throughout the story. This only serves to demonstrate how easily any culturally important text (especially one that is revered by many) can be misused to give a false credence and authority to world-views borne out of hatred and destructive human agendas rather than any divine ones. Ward's (2004: 2) criticism of people who use the Bible like Stryker does is worth repeating:

> Their view is selective, because it accepts only some biblical teachings, and it interprets them in an implausibly literalistic sense. It is restrictive, because it is does not permit alternative interpretations . . . and it is exclusive, because it seems to interpret the Bible in a way that excludes most people from the saving love of God.

One message for children here is the need to analyse arguments critically for oneself rather than being swayed by a charismatic delivery of them: such an ability can serve as a good guard against being exploited or controlled or radicalized by others, especially those who set themselves up as self-proclaimed mouthpieces for the word of God. It is Magneto who succinctly puts what is really going on:

> Once more, genocide in the name of God. A story as old as the race.
> (Claremont 1982/2007: 141)

Eventually, after the Purifiers are defeated, and in a televised public meeting led by Stryker, it falls to Cyclops to give the story's overarching moral plea:

Cyclops: Thanks to you – and people like you – mutants live in fear every day of our lives. And sometimes those lives are very short. Less than a week ago, two children in Connecticut were *murdered*, Stryker – condemned solely for an accident of birth. Would you do that to someone because of the colour of their skin or their beliefs?

Stryker: I do nothing, Cyclops. I am an instrument of the Lord. And whatever a man's color or beliefs, he is still *human*. Those children – and you X-Men – are *not!*

Cyclops: Says who? You? What makes your link with heaven any stronger than mine? We have unique gifts – but no more so, and no more special, than those granted a physician or physicist, or philosopher or athlete. It could be due to an accident or nature or divine providence, who's to say? Are arbitrary labels more important than the way we live our lives, what we're supposed to be more important than what we actually *are?!*

(Claremont 1982/2007: 172)

What comes over above all is the importance of respecting common humanity and the danger that results when any particular group of people are singled out as less than human or as human beings of a lower value in some way. The story (and, indeed, the entire canon of X-Men narratives) demonstrates that if common humanity and individual character and worth are not recognized or respected, then we are on the slippery slope towards committing all kinds of oppressive and atrocious actions towards our fellow human beings, simply because we do not recognize them as such.

There is also a sustained insistence that human beings should be treated and respected as individual persons first and foremost, without any prejudice or discrimination resulting from any crude group definitions that might be applied to them; in fact, that all people should have the right to develop and express their individual identities freely. This can be seen in Cyclop's and Professor X's entreaties above, and it is demonstrated in the astonishingly diverse range of characters and personalities that make up the X-Men at different times; but perhaps this issue finds most expression with the character Mystique, who starts as one of Professor X's X-Men, but ends up as one of Magneto's Brotherhood of Mutants, precisely because of Magneto's valuing of her natural self, as will be seen.

Magneto and his Brotherhood of Mutants

The film *X-Men* (2000) starts off by showing the young Jewish boy Eric Lensherr (we know he is Jewish because of the large yellow Star of David on his father's clothing) being herded into a Nazi concentration camp and forcefully separated from his parents. The scene is faithfully recreated at the beginning of *X-Men: First Class* (2011), only this time it continues with the execution of his mother, and the whole film revolves around the grown-up Eric Lensherr's pursuit of revenge for what was done to him and his family. In one early scene he visits a bank that holds ex-Nazi bank accounts with a block of Nazi gold: 'This gold is what remains of my people. Melted from their possessions. Torn from their teeth. This is blood money. And you're going to help me find the bastards responsible for it' (Vaughan 2011).

For Eric Lensherr, the Nazis have served to reveal humanity's true character. Humanity is evil and cruel, composed of utter hatred and able to commit the most atrocious of acts. Lensherr takes the emergence of mutants – or *Homo superior*, as Stryker and others term them – as a sign that the time of *Homo sapiens* is over, and that there will be little loss in the passing of such a perverse, malicious and hate-filled species. For him, evolution will follow its natural course, and *Homo superior* will replace *Homo sapiens* as the dominant species on planet Earth (much as Cro-Magnon man replaced Neanderthals).

Because, for him, humanity is an evil and harmful species, and one that has run its last race anyway, Lensherr has no compunction about killing human beings if they get in the way of his agenda – something that divides him utterly from Charles Xavier. In fact, it is finally Lensherr's dealing of death to the man who killed his mother that prevents their early friendship from developing further, even though they retain a grudging respect for one another. Professor X, like Superman and Batman before him, will not use death as a weapon to achieve his aims.

Once Lensherr (now Magneto) has accomplished his revenge, he sets off on his agenda for all other X-Men stories, which is to make the world safe for mutantkind. The harsh measures he is willing to take to accomplish this mean that he and the X-Men are opposed to each other (except for the few times that they cautiously and temporarily join forces against a common threat, such as Stryker and his Purifiers). The X-Men desire to live in peace and equality with the rest of humanity, while Magneto regards humanity as the inferior species and acts accordingly.

Three of his actions stand out. The first is his creation of the Brotherhood of Mutants, a group composed of like-minded mutants who believe themselves to be superior to the rest of mankind. They also, like all groups who believe that they are innately superior to other peoples, believe they are beyond having any moral duties to anyone outside their particular group, and so can treat them in any way they wish. The Brotherhood of Mutants consider the rest of humanity to be a threat to their own existence, but, unlike the X-Men, respond to this perceived threat with their own aggression and punishment.

Magneto's second action is to (forcefully) take command of a small island state near South Africa called Genosha, and set this up as a homeland for mutants – with him as absolute ruler, of course. (This establishment of a homeland for one particular group finds echoes in human history, with different peoples claiming different geographical territories as exclusively for themselves, with all the problems that emerge.) Cyclops takes him to task for this, but Magneto is not short of a confident reply:

> Magneto: Look at yourselves, risking your lives for a humanity that would rather see you behind bars, or dead. Why do you persist?
> Cyclops: Is your way any better? A mutant dictatorship?
> Magneto: Do not take that tone with me, boy. I have lived under a dictatorship – and seen my family butchered by its servants. When I rule, it will be for the betterment of all. Contentment breeds tranquillity – discontent, rebellion. Therefore, I shall ensure the one by eliminating the root causes of the other: hunger, poverty, disease, war. The freedoms lost will not be noticed . . . and the material benefits should more than balance the scales.
>
> (Claremont 1982/2007: 162)

This, of course, has echoes of Jarvis Kord in the Batman story *Fall of the Blue Beetle!* (see Chapter 8). Older children could consider the very notion of a 'benevolent dictator' and explore whether such a thing could ever be possible or desirable (or, indeed, whether it has ever existed in, say, English history, under certain monarchs). They could also explore the promises offered by dictators who turned out to be anything but benevolent in practice, and, perhaps, see why so many people in different nations have fallen for them at different times.

Finally, there is Magneto's quite worthy encouragement to all mutants to be themselves and be proud of their mutations as defining parts of their nature. This is clearly seen in *X-Men: First Class* through Magneto's relationship with Raven (Mystique) Darkhölme. Mystique is a shape-changer who has a naturally blue and textured skin. She is very self-conscious of this and chooses to look like a 'normal' – if very pretty – young woman. She is initially taken in by a very young Charles Xavier and passes herself off as his sister. Early on in the film she criticizes one of his sayings:

> Mystique: 'Mutant – and proud!' That's only with pretty mutations, or invisible ones like yours. If you are a freak, better hide.
>
> (Vaughan 2011)

Later in the film she talks with Hank McCoy, whose own mutation has led to him having what he sees as deformed feet:

> Mystique: Look at all we've achieved this week – all we will achieve. We are different, but we shouldn't be trying to fit into society. Society should aspire to be more like us. Mutant – and proud!

McCoy: It behoves me to tell you that even if we save the world tomorrow [*which they do*] and mutations are accepted into society, my feet, your natural blue form, will never be described as 'beautiful'.

(Vaughan 2011)

This unexpected reply affects Mystique's confidence, but it is Eric Lensherr who restores it when she visits his room. He insists on seeing 'the *real* Raven' (Vaughan 2011), by which he means Mystique without her habitual disguise as a normal, pretty girl, and when she tentatively reveals herself to him he tells her how beautiful she is. At the end of the film she leaves Professor X, whom she thinks has never been comfortable with her natural form, and joins Lensherr's embryonic Brotherhood, her final words to Professor X being 'Mutant – and proud'.

Later (in *X2: X-Men United*) a more grown-up version of Mystique meets Nightcrawler, who has been persecuted for his appearance all his life. Nightcrawler approaches her:

Nightcrawler: Excuse me. They say you can imitate anybody, even their voices.
Mystique: [*Impersonating him*] Even their voices.
Nightcrawler: Then why not stay in disguise all the time? You know – look like everyone else?
Mystique: Because we shouldn't have to.

(Singer 2003)

Mystique is quite right of course; neither she nor anyone else whose identity and appearance are different from others should not have to conceal or negate who they are in order to be accepted or fit into society. One of the good things that Magneto does is promote the right to be oneself and not have to face prejudice because of this. His Brotherhood of Mutants exists partly because its members find an acceptance within the group that is denied to them by the wider world. 'At their core both of my *X-Men* movies are about bigotry and intolerance' said their director, Bryan Singer (reported by Waddell 2012), and the character of Mystique and the harsh steps taken by Magneto to protect and promote what he sees as mutant dignity and rights invite children to explore the issue of what moral limits there should be to the preservation of the necessary right to one's own identity, and how this right interplays with the rights of others.

Learning ideas

This chapter has shown how the X-Men characters and narratives explore themes of rejection, fear, prejudice, equality, inclusion and standing up for one's rights. Teaching about these significant themes cannot be done well in an over-simple manner, and is probably best done over time so there are opportunities to explore issues deeply and develop sustained and genuinely thoughtful conversations, and also the establishment of an atmosphere where children feel secure and enabled to discuss such potentially emotive themes with the entitlement of respectful freedom of speech. Using stories and scenarios related to the X-Men can give rise to teaching opportunities that allow children the safety to explore these significant themes in relation to fictional characters and fictional groupings of humanity; in other words, without fearing that they are likely to step on someone's toes or cause unnecessary offence. Once the themes identified in this chapter have begun to be explored in relation to the X-Men, then the conversations that follow can extend to real-life scenarios, whether to do with Citizenship, PSHE, History, RE, Ethics or Philosophy. Here are just a few possible learning prompts; the possibilities are probably endless, but all can be seen as essentially to do with advancing children's moral education. The possibilities suggested here are really on a sliding scale – they can be carried out fairly simply for the younger children or explored in great depth, even as far as master's or PhD level in some cases.

Mutate into a superhero!

Children could be asked to identify some specific abilities of theirs that they are most proud of and take delight in. They could then pretend that these abilities grew through mutation into highly developed and special versions of themselves. What powers would result, and what would the children do with them? How would they use their special mutated powers for good?

Create your own themed X-Men!

Children could imagine themselves as Professor X, tasked with recruiting the next roster of the X-Men. Each Professor X would be given a theme to base his or her choice around: for example, one group of X-Men might all have to have mutations based on the five senses, another group on ways of physically moving, another on scientific forces, another on types of animal, and so on. These varied groups could then find expression by being drawn, or danced, or dramatized, as well as being given suitably creative and evocative names.

Mutant – and proud!

Children could be asked to create self-portraits. These would be not so much pictorial representations (though these could certainly be included) as expressions of identity: their tastes, their likes and dislikes, their ambitions, their loyalties, their hobbies, the type of books or stories they enjoy – essentially their feelings about their relationship to the rest of the world. Mystique could be used as an example of a person who starts off by hiding who she really is but ends up proud and empowered to be herself.

Genosha

Magneto established what he advertised as a haven for mutants. Children could be invited to identify what geographical, social, economic and ethical features of a community would allow it to be regarded as a haven, and design any of its aspects, from architecture or artistic life to political or legal system.

A challenging (to any depth one likes) extension of this for older children and students would be to explore notions of a 'homeland'. Using the idea of Genosha as a starting point, children could explore real-life 'homelands' such as areas reserved for Native American Indians or Aborigines, as well as ideas about homeland and nationality. They could start to ask questions about whether and to what extent cultural groups should have their own dedicated spaces and to what extent they should be integrated together. Eventually, for much older students, this could lead to critical exploration of historical, political and possibly religious movements dedicated to the establishment of culturally specific or culturally determined states and areas of the world (the British Empire? Israel as a Jewish state? The various theocracies around the world?) and the various benefits and problems related to these. The issue that gets raised in the end is to what extent human beings integrate or stay within their home cultures – in other words, to what extent humans are tribal beings, whether to do with religion, nationality, language, cultural values, fashion, sexual behaviour, economic status, type of housing, or even football club affiliation. How does any dominant cultural group affect and relate with the other cultural groups within the community?

The rights and treatment of different species and groups

Magneto and his Brotherhood of Mutants regard *Homo superior* as literally superior to *Homo sapiens*. In the same manner, real-life human beings often act and think as if *Homo sapiens* was the key species on Earth. Children could be asked to suggest some rights that species *other* than human should be acknowledged as having. They could then be asked to draw up some principles for how they should treat animals, and articulate what duties of care they should have towards them.

An extension of this for older children and students would be for them to carry out the equivalent exercise, only this time consider the rights that different groups of people should have, such as convicted criminals, or disabled people, or even children. One very productive way of doing this is for the learners to work in small groups and draw up three lists: the rights that they all agree that the group of people under discussion should have, the rights that they all agree that the group of people under discussion should *not* have, and the possible rights that they cannot reach any agreement over. The discussions should be very thought-provoking, with the third list being the one that sparks most thought and discussion.

Responding to fear, hatred and prejudice

Professor X and his X-Men work for the establishment of peace, harmony and equality between humans and mutants, even though the human population seems to victimize them in oppressive, hateful and often violent ways. Magneto and his Brotherhood, on the other hand, believe in striking back and securing their own safety and well-being through violent means if necessary, and are not interested in the establishment of peace, harmony or equality between the two groups at all. Which group is right? Children could explore this issue is many creative ways, ranging from debate about moral principle and the most desirable outcome to be worked towards to dramatic story-telling to pairs of children role-playing being members of each group and trying to convince the other why their particular group has got it right. Another way of doing this would be for children to read Claremont's *The Uncanny X-Men: God Loves, Man Kills* (1982/2007) properly (or be guided through it by the teacher) and extract the various characters' points of view and rationales for themselves.

A challenging extension of this for older children and students would be to study real-life statements from various historical and contemporary individuals and organizations that seem to take one line of approach or the other – for example, Martin Luther King's famous 'I have a dream' speech, President Lincoln's inaugural address to the American people, or carefully chosen extracts of more militant points of view. The children could try to iden-tify what ethical and social principles and assumptions can be found in such texts and articulate their critical and moral responses to these. Are there any circumstances when any group is allowed to use violence against any other or not? If they were mutants in the X-Men's universe, would they join Professor X or Magneto? Why?

Conclusion: The merit of superheroes and superhero play

We have seen how, at their best, superheroes and their narratives explore deep moral and ethical concerns, from what it is to be a good character to the importance of working towards justice, happiness and the greater good for all. We have found that superheroes and other characters in their worlds can exemplify admirable virtues and demonstrate their good moral principles in the way they respond to moral conflicts and difficulties. We have explored several superhero narratives that really consist of dramatizations of a range of moral approaches and scenarios as well as the consequences that result from choices that different characters make. All these narratives invite (and sometimes require) their readers and viewers to exercise moral reasoning and consider their own moral values in quite considerable ways.

Superheroes (and many non-superpowered characters in their narratives) serve to give voice to the moral principles and considerations that lie at the heart of the scenarios they find themselves in. They demonstrate through their choices and actions that it is important to try to improve the lot of other people and secure their safety, opportunity and fair treatment. Without exception superheroes take a stand – and attempt to act out that stand with integrity in an unselfish manner. While doing so, superheroes exemplify confidence in their own identity and capability – the capability, really, of avoiding doing nothing in the face of injustice. They can be profoundly helpful and stirring role models for children, as they stand for unlimited possibility and the overcoming of all forms of evil, hardship and pain. They all have different approaches, priorities, and methods (which can lead to conflict and disagreement between them) but they all strive for good and believe in the virtue of goodness. They are, in other words, heralds of the much-desired happy ending, where every difficulty, conflict, doubt and rejection by others is overcome; at least, they will not give up until such a thing is achieved.

At the same time, superheroes are *fun*, which is what draws many children to them in the first place. Sheer delight can be found in their dynamic movements, dramatic and flattering costumes, gadgets, cornball speeches to each other, the interplay between different characters, their bold and confident expression of identity, and the element of KA-*POW!* – which is really shorthand for the joy of life. Superheroes fly, they swoop, they crawl up walls, they leap over buildings in a single bound, they get through doors that are impossible to get through, they escape death-traps with jaunty quips and much pizzazz. They and their adventures contain many tongue-in-cheek elements; take the entirety of Adam West's wonderful *Batman* television series of the 1960s, and also this more recent example:

> Green Lantern: A one-way *pocket teleporter* pre-programmed with the *coordinates* to a *black hole*. Seriously? *Why . . .?*
> Batman: In case I ever *needed* it.
> Green Lantern: But . . . Y'know what? Forget I *asked*.
>
> (Walker 2011: 25)

This exuberance makes superheroes very attractive to many, and also makes the moral themes of their narratives digestible and accessible for children. Part of the fun of engaging with the X-Men and all the deep and difficult themes explored in their stories, for example, is watching Wolverine light a cigar on the wreck of a burning car or seeing him flash his claws menacingly and say something like 'Is that all you got, bub?', or watching Professor X raise his fingers to his temple and close his eyes, wondering if he will be able to extract the location of the bomb from the villain's head in time to stop it going off, or Magneto flick his wrist and cause a convoy of cars to fly to one side and crash in a heap. How fabulous and empowering to be able to do any of these things!

Superheroes and their narratives exist on a sliding scale. To begin with, there are the overtly 'educational' superheroes particularly designed with very young children in mind, such as Tree Fu Tom and Tommy Zoom. Each of these superheroes has a particular and deliberate focus. Tree Fu Tom has been deliberately designed to promote young children's physical development (now a Primary Area of Learning and Development within the EYFS) as a large element of the show is the frequent entreaty of Tom to the audience to help him make Tree Fu magic by joining in particular sequences of movement with him. According to the BBC (2012), which produces and broadcasts the show:

> The movements of the Tree Fu spells that children are encouraged and guided to copy are designed to help teach children, and allow them to practise, as many as 12 key developmentally crucial skills/ attributes that they need for all future movement. The spells are linked sequences of simple 'foundation movements', the building blocks of all co-ordinated movement. They are designed . . . to enhance gross and fine motor skills, strength, balance, co-ordination and neurological development.

The BBC (2012) also states that the Tree Fu Tom series has been designed to help children learn about things such as friendship, leadership and simple moral and emotional issues.

The same could be said for Tommy Zoom, another superhero produced particularly for pre-school children. Tommy Zoom, along with his dog Daniel (who is the narrator and moral conscience of his stories), exists in two forms: as a real-life boy involved in real-life gentle family situations, and as a cartoon superhero. Each Tommy Zoom story begins by showing the real-life version pausing to consider a simple moral decision. 'What should Tommy do?' asks Daniel each episode, before repeating the two choices of the particular episode; for example, whether Tommy should persist in a food fight with his baby sister Sam that is wrecking the kitchen or 'clear up the terrible mess' (Allen 2007). The scene then shifts to a related story about Tommy Zoom and his arch-enemy Polluto (who has a comic cat called Smog, a counterpoint to Daniel) – in this instance in a café where Polluto sells 'More than you can eat' meals. Polluto says:

> The recipe for world domination is as simple as Bish Bash Bosh. Bish! Take one large planet. Bash! Chuck on masses and masses of delicious tasty food. Bosh! Mix it all up and leave to rot! Oh, disgusting! With all that smelly waste covering the Earth, there'll be no room to grow fresh food! And the world will be mine!

> (Allen 2007)

One can see by the name of the villain what the overarching theme of the show is. Every episode involves some danger to the cleanliness or health of the environment, which Tommy and Daniel always overcome in humorous and often physically silly ways.

Tommy Zoom serves to introduce moral and environmental themes to young children in an easily accessible and funny manner, and it can be seen how readily lessons featuring Tommy Zoom could be created to help with early learning in Understanding the World, Science, Geography or Citizenship, just as Tree Fu Tom could be utilized to help promote physical development. In fact, the lovely device 'What should Tommy do?' could be used to help young children explore simple moral and behavioural choices that they are likely to come across while in any particular class.

As well as these deliberately educational superheroes there are those who are there, it seems, purely to entertain. For young children the key example that comes to mind is *The Superhero Squad Show* (2008 onwards), which is a delightful, slapstick and often extremely funny and affectionate parody of Marvel superheroes. The heroes all live in Superhero City and the villains, led by Doctor Doom, live in the neighbouring Villainville. The main dynamic of the stories is that the powerful 'infinity sword' has been smashed into fragments and the villains are after these 'fractals', which, if they put them all together again, will somehow lead to their unspecified advantage. The heroes, therefore, have to prevent these things falling into their hands. In other words, this is the harmless plot device that allows for many comic confrontations and physically ridiculous adventures to take place. The entire show is completely tongue-in-cheek, with individual episodes given titles such as *Pedicure and the Facial of Doom!* (Pursell 2010) and dialogue such as the following from *Too Many Wolverines!* (2010):

> Iron Man: Uh oh! I smell clone!
> Thor: Aha! You like it? Manly! It's called Ragnarok Spit.
> Iron Man: [*Sighs*] Not 'cologne' – 'clone'! As in cheap copies of the original.
> Thor: Aye, thou hast busted me royally: 'tis a foul fragrance – [*Aside*] I got it at Odinmart.
>
> (Son 2010)

For older children and adults the example of superheroes as entertainment that most comes to mind is the phenomenally popular *Avengers Assemble* film of 2012. This upbeat film drew the following review:

> What do you get if you cross a Norse god-king with an ego the size of the planet, a nervy scientist boffin with gigantic anger issues, a super-soldier in a silly costume and a genius billionaire playboy with flying armour? Arguments, obviously. With great power comes great banter in writer/director Joss Whedon's blockbuster multiplier, which isn't the best superhero movie ever – but might well be the funniest.
>
> (Crocker 2012: 59)

These types of superhero narrative are worth mentioning simply because they are essentially *playful*. Much of children's superhero play manifests itself at this level of fun and happy physicality; it consists of chase games, constructing vehicles, hideouts and devices to be incorporated into the imaginary scenarios, dressing up and pretending to swoop, leap, fight, rescue and save people like superheroes do. Alternately, it consists of virtual games such as *Lego Batman* and many other hand-held and online variants that take superheroes and put them in scenarios that require children to get through levels with their problem-solving skills; for example, the game *Spider-Man: Friend or Foe* (Activision Publishing 2007) for Nintendo DS and other devices requires children to solve mathematical problems, break codes, find routes, and so on.

What these types of stories and play do is invite children into a secure, child-friendly and ultimately joyous interaction with superheroes that has a great potential to lead to a deeper engagement with the final type of superhero narratives – the ones that quite deliberately explore deep moral and emotional themes (such as those discussed within this book). Children who have enjoyed the *Avengers Assemble!* film (Whedon 2012) can go on to see *The Amazing Spider-Man* (Webb 2012), with its heart-wrenching and highly emotional portrayal of the death of Peter Parker's Uncle Ben, or immerse themselves in X-Men stories about equality, prejudice and the innate goodness or evil that might be found in mankind. Eventually they might find themselves engaging with quite profound narratives such as the astonishing and moving *The World's Greatest Super-Heroes* (Dini and Ross 2005/2010), which takes us back to where it all started in *Superman #1*, with the superheroes in the story trying to work against – not supervillains or unlikely sci-fi events – but real-life evils:

> And so: Superman decides he's going to solve world hunger. Of *course* he would. The idea is so obvious you wonder why you haven't seen it before. Batman strikes at the actual core causes of crime – the unrelenting poverty and desperation that haunts the urban poor. Wonder Woman assumes the daunting task of changing what she sees as the often degrading and oppressed role of women in some cultures. Captain Marvel, that perennial man-boy, delves into the plight of disabled children. The Justice League band together to combat . . . a *disease*.
>
> (Kidd 2005/2010: 4)

Unsurprisingly, despite these superheroes' remarkable powers and abilities, they all fail – defeated by both the scale of the problems and the wilful flaws of humanity, which seem to render it incapable of significant change or necessary unselfishness. At least, they all fail when trying to accomplish something on a grand scale. None of them, however, give up; and all of them continue to work productively towards their goal at a more modest, human level. Nor do they lose their faith in humanity. As Wonder Woman says:

> I will always be Wonder Woman when the need arises . . . Until then, a new role awaits me. That of an ordinary woman . . . who strives to do her best, armed with only a loving heart and a deep belief in the sometimes hidden, but always inherent, goodness of the people around her.
>
> (Dini and Ross 2005/2010: 242)

They do not give up. They do not let go of what they think is right, nor stop striving to achieve it. And they believe in *us*: in the child or adult engaging with their stories. This is the mark of the superhero role model and the essence of every good superhero narrative. One of the proper and most long-standing aims of education is to develop children's and students' *good character*, and if, as first Aristotle and later O'Hear and Sidwell (2009: 14) suggest, good character is not 'merely knowing the good, but acting well', then superheroes are among the most potent fictional examples of this to be found in our shared culture.

Several learning ideas have been suggested in this book. All of these – while productive – are somewhat limited in that it is not the case that instant and short-term exposure to something leads to instant or thorough under-standing (see Bruner 1963). Deep and significant understanding comes from extensive and repeated engagement with and high-quality cultural expression of ideas. This applies to the possible moral understandings and sensitivities available through superhero stories and characters too. It is quite possible for children to engage with superheroes, superhero play and superhero activities superficially or temporarily, and much of the goodness potentially on offer might pass them by. At the same time, an ongoing absorption of superhero narratives and themes has the potential to deeply inform and impact upon children's developing moral sensibilities, and it is in the hope of promoting such a thing that this book has been written. After all, as Garrett (2005: 165) states beautifully:

> When we read comics month after month, go to movies featuring Spider-Man, Batman, the X-Men, it's only partly to see the fight scenes and special effects. We also go because we believe – in some way we may not even consciously acknowledge – in the moral and dramatic fitness of the stories. The characters we love represent something different from the characters who oppose them. There is good and there is evil, and we want to see how good will ultimately triumph.

If Garrett is correct about our key motive for engaging and playing with superheroes and their stories, then perhaps Wonder Woman's faith in humanity's inherent goodness, like Superman's, and Jor-El's, and Professor X's before her, is justified. Superheroes are only a little element of the entire worthy culture of thought, literature and art that surrounds us, but they are a popular one, and superheroes have great scope to be used with children to help ensure that we can eventually rise above whatever inside us causes the existence of Nazis and all other oppressors and tyrants in the first place. Perhaps, one day, Magneto will be proven wrong.

Children: You really saved the day, Batman.
Batman: I couldn't have done it without your help, kids. Thanks. And thank *you*, Steven Popper. You helped me save *America's* greatest symbol of *freedom*. GOOD WORK!!
Steven Popper: It's like my *Bat-Buddy* always says, 'You don't need a *cape* and a *costume* to be a hero'. Oh yeah, he also wishes everybody a safe and happy *Fourth of July*. This is Steven Popper signing off.
(Waid et al. 1994: 32)

References

Activision Publishing (2007) *Spider-Man: Friend or Foe*: Uxbridge: Activision UK Ltd.

Adamson, P. (2008) *Unicef Report Card 8: The Childcare Transition*. Florence: Unicef Innocenti Research Centre. Available at: http://www.unicef-irc.org/publications/pdf/rc8_eng.pdf. Accessed 20 September 2010.

Allen, M. (2007) *Food Fight* in *Tommy Zoom*. London: BBC Worldwide.

Aquinas, T. (2009) *The Summa Theologica of St. Thomas Aquinas*. London: BiblioLife.

Aristotle (2004) *The Nichomachean Ethics* (transl. J.A.K. Thomson). London: Penguin.

Athey, C. (1990) *Extending Thought in Young Children*. London: Paul Chapman Publishing.

Baker-Fletcher, G.K. (2000) *Dirty Hands: Christian Ethics in a Morally Ambiguous World*. Minneapolis: Fortress Press.

Bandura, A., Ross, S.A. and Ross, D. (1961) Transmission of aggression through imitation of aggressive models. *Journal of Abnormal and Social Psychology*, 63(3): 575–582.

Bandura, A., Ross, S.A. and Ross, D. (1963) Vicarious reinforcement and imitative learning. *Journal of Abnormal Psychology*, 67(6): 601–607.

Baron-Cohen, S. (2004) *The Essential Difference*. London: Penguin.

Bauer, K.L. and Dettore, E. (1997) Superhero play: What's a teacher to do? *Early Childhood Education Journal*, 25(1): 17–23.

BBC (2012) *Tree Fu Tom: Aimed at Assisting Child Development*. Available at http://www.bbc.co.uk/cbeebies/grownups/programme/tree-fu-tom. Accessed 16 August 2012.

BBC News (2009) Toy weapons 'help boys to learn', 19 May. Available: http://news.bbc.co.uk/1/hi/education/7163741.stm. Accessed 23 March 2010.

BBC News (2011) Five minutes with: John Humphrys, 13 August. Available at: http://www.bbc.co.uk/news/entertainment-arts-14510149. Accessed 6 June 2012.

Beechen, A. (2009) *Invasion of the Secret Santas! Batman: The Brave and the Bold Episode 4*. California: Warner Bros Entertainment.

Berkowitz, S., Burnett, A. and Heinberg, A. (2011–) *Batman Live World Arena Tour*. New York: Water Lane Productions in association with Warner Bros Consumer Products and DC Entertainment.

Bettleheim, B. (1976) *The Uses of Enchantment*. London: Penguin.

Bjorklund, D.F. and Pellegrini, A.D. (2002) *The Origins of Human Nature: Evolutionary Developmental Psychology*. Washington, DC: American Psychological Association.

Bowlby, J. (1953/1965) *Child Care and the Growth of Love* (2nd edition). Harmondsworth: Penguin.

Bowlby, J. (1969) *Attachment and Loss Vol. 1: Attachment*. New York: Basic Books.

Bowlby, J. (1979/2000) *The Making and Breaking of Affectional Bonds*. London: Routledge.

Brennert, A. and Giordano, D. (1981) *To Kill a Legend* in *Detective Comics #500*. New York: DC Comics.

Brodkin, A. (2003) When superheroes invade. *Early Childhood Today Journal*, 18(2): 38–41.

Bruner, J.S. (1962/1979) *On Knowing: Essays for the Left Hand*. Cambridge, MA: Harvard University Press.

Bruner, J.S. (1963) Looking at the curriculum. *Educational Courier*, 33(3): 18–26.

Bruner, J.S. (1986) *Actual Minds, Possible Worlds*. Cambridge, MA: Harvard University Press.

Bruner, J.S. (1990) *Acts of Meaning*, Cambridge, MA: Harvard University Press.

Bruner, J.S. (2006) *In Search of Pedagogy Vol. 2*. London: Routledge.

Burnett, A. (1993) *Batman: Mask of the Phantasm*. California: Warner Bros Entertainment.

Burnett, A. (2011) *Green Lantern: First Flight*. California: Warner Bros Animation.

Campbell, J. (1949/1993) *The Hero with a Thousand Faces*. London: Fontana Press.

Capizzi, D. and Timm, B. (2007) *Superman: Doomsday*. California: Warner Bros Entertainment.

Claremont, C. (1982/2007) *The Uncanny X-Men: God Loves, Man Kills*. Tunbridge Wells: Panini Publishing.

Cohen, D. (2006) *The Development of Play* (3rd edition). London: Routledge.

Coles, R. (1997) *The Moral Intelligence of Children*. London: Bloomsbury.

Connell, R.W. (2005) *Masculinities* (2nd edition). Cambridge: Polity Press.

Cotta Vaz, M. (1989) *Tales of the Dark Knight*. London: Futura.

Cowsill, A. (2012) *King of Chaos* in *The Joker: DC Chess Collection #2*. London: Eaglemoss.

Crocker, J. (2012) *Avengers Assemble: Earth's Funniest Heroes* in *Total Film #194*. London: Future Publishing.

Daniels. L. (1991) *Marvel: Five Fabulous Decades of the World's Greatest Comics*. London: Virgin Press.

DC Comics (2005) *Being Lois Lane*, DVD documentary. California: Warner Bros Entertainment.

DeFalco, T. (2008) 1960s. In C. Saunders, H. Scott, J. March and A. Dougall (eds), *Marvel Chronicle: A Year by Year History*. London, Dorling Kindersley.

Department for Children, Schools and Families (2008a) *The Early Years Foundation Stage*. Nottingham: DCSF Publications.

Department for Children, Schools and Families (2008b) *Practice Guidance for the Early Years Foundation Stage*. Nottingham: DCSF Publications.

Department for Education (2012) *Statutory Framework for the Early Years Foundation Stage*, DfE 00023-2012. Runcorn: DfE.

Department for Education and Employment and Qualifications and Curriculum Authority (1999) *The National Curriculum Handbook for Primary Teachers in England*. London: HMSO.

Derek, S.C. and Dixon, B. (1992) *Cat Scratch Fever: The Animated Batman*. New York: Warner Bros.

Dini, P. and Ross, A. (2005/2010) *The World's Greatest Super-Heroes*. New York: DC Comics.

Dixon, B. (1990) *Playing Them False: A Study of Children's Toys, Games and Puzzles*. Stoke-on-Trent: Trentham Books.

Duska, R. and Whelan, M. (1977) *Moral Development: A Guide to Piaget and Kohlberg*. Dublin: Gill & Macmillan.

Dweck, C.S. (2000) *Self-Theories: Their Role in Motivation, Personality and Development*. Hove: Psychology Press.

Edens, M. (1992) *Night of the Sentinels* in *X-Men: Season 1 Volume 1*. London: Marvel Entertainment/Clear Vision.

Edens, M. (1993/2009) *X-Men: Till Death Do Us Part*. London: Marvel Entertainment/ Clear Vision.

Eldridge, S. (1999) *Twenty Things Adopted Kids Wish Their Adoptive Parents Knew*. New York: Dell Publishing.

Engel, S. (1999) *The Stories Children Tell*. New York: W.H. Freeman.

Engelhart, S. (1973) *Finally, Shuma-Gorath!* in *Marvel Premiere #10*. New York: Marvel Comics Group.

Evans, C.S. (2005) Why should superheroes be good? Spider-Man, the X-Men, and Kierkegaard's double danger. In T. Morris and M. Morris (eds), *Superheroes and Philosophy*. Chicago: Open Court.

Feiffer, J. (1965) *The Great Comic Book Heroes*. New York: Dial Press.

Fergus, M., Ostby, H., Marcum, A. and Holloway, M. (2008) *Iron Man*. California: Marvel Entertainment.

Fingeroth, D. (2004) *Superman on the Couch*. London: Continuum.

Fisch, S. (2012) *Help Wanted* in *Batman: The Brave and the Bold #24*. London: Titan Comics.

Frost, M. and France, M. (2007) *Fantastic Four*. California: Marvel/Twentieth Century Fox Home Entertainment.

Galloway, J.T., Jr. (1973) *The Gospel According to Superman*. Philadelphia: A.J. Holman.

Games Workshop (2009) *Space Hulk*. Nottingham: Games Workshop.

Garrett, G. (2005) *Holy Superheroes! Exploring Faith and Spirituality in Comic Books*. Colorado Springs: Pinon Press.

General Teaching Council (2008) *Annual Digest of Statistics: Profiles of Registered Teachers in England* [online]. Available at: http://www.gtce.org.uk/shared/contentlibs/gtc/141488/201080/stat_digest_08. Accessed: 1 December 2008.

Gilligan, C. (1982) *In a Different Voice*. Cambridge, MA: Harvard University Press.

Gough, A. and Millar, M. (2002) *Rosetta: Smallville (Season 2)*. California: Warner Bros Entertainment.

Gray, A. and Maynard, J. (2008) *Wonder Woman: The Amazonian Princess*, documentary included in G. Simone and M. Jelenic (2009) *Wonder Woman*. California: Warner Bros Entertainment.

Gray, S. (2012) *Refuge* in *X-Men First Class Annual 2012*. Tunbridge Wells: Panini Publishing.

Groos, K. (1901) *The Play of Man*. London: Heinemann.

Gurian, M. (2002) *Boys and Girls Learn Differently! A Guide for Teachers and Parents*. San Francisco, Jossey-Bass.

Gurian, M. and Stevens, K. (2007) *The Minds of Boys: Saving Our Boys from Falling Behind in School and Life*. San Francisco: Jossey-Bass.

Haney, B. and Dillin, D. (2008) *Superman/Batman: Saga of the Super Sons!* London: Titan Books.

Haney, B., Dillin, D. and Colletta, V. (1974) *Evil in Paradise* in *World's Finest Comics #222*. New York: National Periodical Publications.

Hermans, H.J.M., Kempen, H.J.G. and van Loon, R.J.P. (1992) The dialogical self: Beyond individualism and rationalism. *American Psychologist*, 47: 23–33.

Hoffman, M.L. (1970) Moral development. In P.H. Mussen (ed.), *Carmichael's Manual of Child Psychology* (Vol. 2). New York: Wiley.

Hoffman, M.L. (2000) *Empathy and Moral Development: Implications for Caring and Justice*. New York: Cambridge University Press.

Holland, P. (1999) Just pretending. *Language Matters Journal*, Spring: 2–5.

Holland, P. (2003) *We Don't Play with Guns Here*. Maidenhead: Open University Press.

Hoskin, R. (2011) *Out of Reach* in *Marvel: Spiderman & Friends #53*. Tunbridge Wells: Panini Comics.

Inglis, F. (1993) *Cultural Studies*. Oxford: Blackwell.

James, A. (2007) *Teaching the Male Brain: How Boys Think, Feel and Learn in School* (3rd edition). London: Sage.

Jarvis, P. (2009) Building 'social hardiness' for life: Rough and tumble play in the early years of primary school. In A. Brock, S. Dodds, P. Jarvis and Y. Olusoga (eds), *Perspectives on Play: Learning for Life*. Harlow: Pearson Education.

Jewett, R. and Lawrence, J.S. (2002) *The Myth of the American Superhero*. Grand Rapids, MI: Eerdmans.

Jorgensen, G. (2006) Kohlberg and Gilligan: Duet or duel? *Journal of Moral Education*, 35(2): 179–196.

Jurgens, D. (1993) *The Death of Superman*. New York: DC Comics.

Kail, R.V. (2010) *Children and Their Development* (5th edition). Upper Saddle River, NJ: Pearson Prentice Hall.

Kane, B. (1940) *The Legend of the Batman – Who He Is And How He Came to Be!* in *Batman #1*, New York: DC Comics.

Kane, B. and Finger, B. (1939) *The Case of the Chemical Syndicate* in *Detective Comics #27*. New York: DC Comics.

Kant, I. (1983) *Groundwork of the Metaphysics of Morals* (transl. H.J. Paton). London: Hutchinson.

Kaveney, R. (2008) *Superheroes! Capes and Crusaders in Comics and Films*. London: I.B. Tauris.

Khan, J. (2006) *Superman for Social Justice*, in *Superman: Cover to Cover*. New York: DC Comics.

Kidd, C. (2005/2010) Introduction: To protect and to serve. In P. Dini and A. Ross, *The World's Greatest Super-Heroes*. New York: DC Comics.

Kohlberg, L. (1984) *The Psychology of Moral Development: The Nature and Validity of Moral Stages*. London: HarperCollins.

Konieczka, C. (2010) *Space Hulk: Death Angel – The Card Game*. Roseville, MN: Fantasy Flight Games.

Krieg, J. (2010) *Fall of the Blue Beetle!: Batman: The Brave and the Bold Episode 8*. California: Warner Bros Entertainment.

Law, S. (2007) *Philosophy*. London: Dorling Kindersley.

Layard, R. and Dunn, J. (2009) *A Good Childhood: Searching for Values in a Competitive Age*. London: Penguin.

Layman, C.S. (2005) Why be a superhero? Why be moral? In T. Morris and M. Morris (eds), *Superheroes and Philosophy*. Chicago: Open Court.

Lee, S. (1967) *The Startling Saga of the Silver Surfer!* in *Fantastic Four #50*. New York: Marvel Comics Group.

Lee, S. and Ditko, S. (1962) *Spiderman: Amazing Fantasy #15*. New York: Marvel.

Lee, S. and Ditko, S. (1963) *The Origin of Dr. Strange: Strange Tales No. 115*. New York: Marvel.

Lee, S. and Kirby, J. (1961) *The Fantastic Four!: Fantastic Four No.1*. Reprinted in S. Lee (1974) *Origins of Marvel Comics*. New York: Simon and Schuster.

Lee, S. and Kirby, J. (1966) *Fantastic Four #55: When Strikes the Silver Surfer!* Reprinted in S. Lee (1974) *Origins of Marvel Comics.* New York: Simon and Schuster.

Levin, D.E. and Carlsson-Paige, N. (2006) *The War Play Dilemma* (2nd edition). New York: Teachers College Press.

Lewald, E. (2011) *X-Men: Ultimate Collection.* London: Marvel Entertainment/Clear Vision.

Lindon, J. (2008) *Safeguarding Children and Young People: Child Protection 0–18 Years* (3rd edition). London: Hodder Education.

Lippa, R.A. (2005) *Gender, Nature and Nurture* (2nd edition). London: Lawrence Erlbaum Associates.

Lowenfield, M. (1967) *Play in Childhood.* New York: Wiley.

Maccoby, E.E. and Jacklin, C.N. (1974) *The Psychology of Sex Differences.* Stanford, CA: Stanford University Press.

MacIntyre, A. (1981) *After Virtue.* London: Duckworth.

MacNaughton, G. (2000) *Rethinking Gender in Early Childhood Education.* London: Paul Chapman Publishing.

Madrid, M. (2009) *The Supergirls: Fashion, Feminism, Fantasy, and the History of Comic Book Heroines.* Ashland, OR: Exterminating Angel Press.

Mallon, B. (2011) *Working with Bereaved Children and Young People.* London: Sage.

Marsh, J. (2000) 'But I want to fly too!': Girls and superhero play in the infant classroom. *Gender and Education Journal,* 12(2): 209–220.

Maslow, A.H. (1943) A theory of human motivation. *Psychological Review,* 50: 370–396.

Maslow, A.H. (1962) *Toward a Psychology of Being.* Princeton, NJ: Van Nostrand.

Maxwell, R.J. and Luber, B. (1951/2005) *Adventures of Superman* [TV series]. California: Warner Bros Entertainment.

Millar, M. (2000) *Superman for the Animals.* New York: DC Comics.

Mitchell, P. and Ziegler, F. (2007) *Fundamentals of Development.* Hove: Psychology Press.

Moench, D. (1993) *Batman: Knightfall* in *Batman #492.* New York: DC Comics.

Morrison, G. (2012) *Batman: The Return: Planet Gotham* in *Batman Legends #52.* London: Titan Magazines.

Murray Parkes, C. (1998) *Bereavement: Studies of Grief in Adult Life* (4th edition). London: Penguin.

Nolan, C. (2005) *Batman Begins.* California: Warner Bros Pictures and Legendary Pictures.

Nolan, C. (2012) *The Dark Knight Rises.* California: Warner Bros Pictures and Legendary Pictures.

Oatley, K., Keltner, D. and Jenkins, J. (2006) *Understanding Emotions* (2nd edition). Oxford: Blackwell.

Ofsted (2011) *Removing Barriers to Literacy* (ref. no. 090237). Manchester: Ofsted.

O'Hara, K.S. (2002) Sam Raimi's heroes. *Screentalk,* May/June.

O'Hear, A. and Sidwell, M. (2009) *The School of Freedom: A Liberal Education Reader from Plato to the Present Day.* Exeter: Imprint-Academic.

Open Mind Productions (2007) *Numberjacks: Standing by to Zoom!* London: Open Mind Productions.

Orczy, E. (1905/2007) *The Scarlet Pimpernel.* New York: Bantam Dell.

Orczy, Baroness E. (1914/2011) *The Laughing Cavalier.* Looe, Cornwall: House of Stratus.

Palmer, S. (2009) *21st Century Boys: How Modern Life is Driving Them Off The Rails and How We Can Get Them Back On Track*. London: Orion.

Parsons, P. (1991) Batman and his audience: The dialectic of culture. In E.E. Pearson and W. Uricchio (eds), *The Many Lives of the Batman*. London: BFI Publishing.

Pellegrini, A.D. (2006) Rough-and-tumble play from childhood through adolescence. In D.P. Fromberg and D. Bergen (eds), *Play from Birth to Twelve: Contexts, Perspectives and Meanings* (2nd edition). Abingdon: Routledge.

Phillips, M. (1998) *All Must Have Prizes*. London: Time Warner.

Piaget, J. (1932/1965) *The Moral Judgement of the Child*. New York: Free Press.

Piaget, J. (1962) *Play, Dreams and Imitation in Childhood*. New York: W.W. Norton.

Piaget, J. and Inhelder, B. (1969) *The Psychology of the Child*. New York: Basic Books.

Picoult, J. (2007) *Wonder Woman: Love and Murder*. New York: DC Comics.

Pinker, S. (1998) *How the Mind Works*: London: Penguin.

Plato (2007) *The Republic* (translated by H.D.P. Lee and D. Lee, 3rd edition). London: Penguin.

Polkinghorne, D. (1988) *Narrative Knowing and the Human Sciences*. Albany: SUNY Press.

Pursell, R. (2010) *Pedicure and the Facial of Doom!* London: Marvel Entertainment/Clear Vision.

Puzo, M., Newman, D., Newman, L. and Benton, R. (1978) *Superman the Movie*. California: Warner Bros Entertainment.

Ratner, B. (2006) *X-Men: The Last Stand*. New York: Twentieth Century Fox.

Reed, E. (2000) *The Genesis of Ethics*. London: Darton, Longman & Todd.

Reeve, C. (2003) *Nothing is Impossible*. London: Arrow Books.

Ridley, M. (2004) *Nature via Nurture*, London: Harper Perennial.

Robbins, T. (1996) *The Great Women Superheroes*. London: Kitchen Sink Press.

Roberts, S. (2012) Batman Ends in Sci Fi Now #68. Bournemouth: Imagine Publishing.

Rogel, R. (1992) *Robin's Reckoning: The Animated Batman*. New York: Warner Bros.

Routh, B. (2006) in DC Comics, *Superman: Cover to Cover*. New York: DC Comics.

Ryall, C. and Tipton, S. (2005) The Fantastic Four as a family: The strongest bond of all. In T. Morris and M. Morris (eds), *Superheroes and Philosophy*. Chicago: Open Court.

Sax, L. (2005) *Why Gender Matters: What Parents and Teachers Need to Know about the Emerging Science of Sex Differences*. New York: Broadway Books.

Sax, L. (2009) *Boys Adrift: The Five Factors Driving the Growing Epidemic of Unmotivated Boys and Underachieving Young Men*. New York: Basic Books.

Siegel, J. and Shuster, J. (1939) *Superman #1*. New York: Detective Comics.

Singer, B. (2000) *X-Men*. New York: Twentieth Century Fox Film Corporation.

Singer, B. (2003) *X2: X-Men United*. New York: Twentieth Century Fox Film Corporation.

Singer, J.L. (1994) Imaginative play and adaptive development. In J.H. Goldstein (ed.), *Toys, Play and Child Development*. Cambridge: Cambridge University Press.

Skelton, B.C. and Francis, B. (2003) *Boys and Girls in the Primary Classroom*. Maidenhead: Open University Press.

Skelton, S. (2006) *The Gospel According to the World's Greatest Superhero*. Eugene, OR: Harvest House.

Smilansky, S. (1990) Sociodramatic play: Its relevance to behaviour and achievement in school. In E. Klugman and S. Smilansky (eds), *Children's Play and Learning: Perspectives and Policy Implications*. New York: Teachers College Press.

Son, E. (2010) *Too Many Wolverines!* London: Marvel Entertainment/Clear Vision.

Stokes, P. (2003) *Philosophy: 100 Essential Thinkers.* London: Arcturus.

Talwar, D. (2012) Daily torment of racism in the classroom, 23 May. Available at http://www.bbc.co.uk/news/education-18150650. Accessed 9 August 2012.

Thompson, B. (2009) Rocking the boat. Unpublished lecture presentation, University of Chichester.

Thorne, B. (1993) *Gender Play: Girls and Boys in Schools.* Buckingham: Open University Press.

TT Games Publishing (2008) *Lego Batman.* California: Warner Bros Interactive Entertainment.

TT Games Publishing (2012) *Lego Batman 2: DC Super Heroes.* California: Warner Bros Interactive Entertainment.

Turiel, E. (2002) *The Culture of Morality.* Cambridge: Cambridge University Press.

Van Evra, J. (2004) *Television and Child Development* (3rd edition). Mahwah, NJ: Lawrence Erlbaum Associates.

Vaughan, M. (2011) *X-Men: First Class.* New York: Twentieth Century Fox Film Corporation.

Vygotsky, L.S. (1978) *Mind in Society: The Development of Higher Psychological Processes.* Cambridge, MA: Harvard University Press.

Waddell, C. (2012) *Time Machine: X-Men 2.* In D. Bradley (ed.), *SFX #225.* Bath: FutureNet.

Wagner, M. (2003) *Batman/Superman/Wonder Woman: Trinity Vol. 11.* New York: DC Comics.

Waid, M. and Ross, A. (2008) *Superman: Kingdom Come.* New York: DC Comics.

Waid, M., Augustyn, B. and Liebman, B. (1994) *Batman and Me!* Special Collector Edition #0006386. New York: DC Comics.

Walker, L.Q. (2011) *The Menace known as Robert!* in *Batman: The Brave and the Bold #19.* London: Titan Comics.

Ward, K. (2002) *God: A Guide for the Perplexed.* Oxford: Oneworld Publications.

Ward, K. (2004) *What the Bible Really Teaches: A Challenge for Fundamentalists,* London: SPCK.

Warrington, M. and Younger, M. (2006) *Raising Boys' Achievement in Primary Schools: Towards an Holistic Approach.* Maidenhead: Open University Press.

Webb, M. (2012) *The Amazing Spider-Man.* California: Columbia Pictures Industries.

Whedon, J. (2012) *Avengers Assemble!* California: Walt Disney Pictures.

White, M.D. (2008) Why doesn't Batman kill the Joker? In M.D. White and R. Arp (eds), *Batman and Philosophy: The Dark Knight of the Soul.* Hoboken, NJ: Wiley.

Winterson, J. (1985/2001) *Oranges Are Not the Only Fruit.* London: Vintage.

Woodhead, C. (2009) *A Desolation of Learning: Is This the Education our Children Deserve?* London: Pencil-Sharp Publishing.

Woolford, A. (2007) *Educational Psychology* (10th edition). London: Pearson.

Index

THE TROUBLE WITH PLAY

Sue Grieshaber and Felicity McArdle

9780335237913 (Paperback)
2010

eBook also available

The Trouble with Play is a radical departure from some of the ideas about play that are held dear by many in early childhood education. For many, play is considered essential to children's development and learning, and is often promoted as a universal and almost magical 'fix'. Although play does have many proven benefits for children, the authors show that play in the early years is not always innocent, fun and natural. Play can also be political and involve morals, ethics, values and power.

Key features:

- Prompts teachers to understand and implement thoughtful approaches to play in the early years
- Uses, practical activities and reflection points
- Encourages discussion about new ways of seeing and thinking about play

www.openup.co.uk

OPEN UNIVERSITY PRESS
McGraw · Hill Education

A–Z OF PLAY IN EARLY CHILDHOOD

Janet Moyles

9780335246380 (Paperback)
2012

eBook also available

This indispensable guide uses a unique glossary format to explore some of the key themes in play in early childhood, many of which regularly arise for students, tutors, parents and practitioners. As well as covering key concepts, theories and influential figures in the field, the book considers important aspects of each construct and highlights the complexity of play in early childhood.

Key features:

- Split into a comprehensive glossary running through elements of play from A–Z, it is a useful, fun and unique companion to understanding children's play
- Original thoughts from well known early years people including Tricia David, Carol Aubrey, Angela Anning and Lilian Katz

www.openup.co.uk